ECHOES
from
RIVER CITY

A *Maine boy comes of age through the*
Great Depression and World War II

PAUL LANDRY

October 24, 2021

To Jimmy & Roz :

With fond rememberances,

— Paul (& Roz)

Echoes from River City
Copyright © 2021 Paul Landry

ISBN: 978-1-63381-263-5

Library of Congress Control Number: 2021907634

Designed and produced by:
Maine Authors Publishing
12 High Street, Thomaston, Maine
www.maineauthorspublishing.com

Printed in the United States of America

This book is dedicated to the memory of my parents:
Ruth Ginsberg Landry and George William Landry, Sr.

PREFACE

It was in the summer several years ago that my partner Roz (Rosamond) suggested I consider writing down the story of my family. There are, of course, interesting happenings and characters in all families, but there were events in mine—for instance how my parents had met—that enchanted her and begged for elaboration and, for my family's benefit, preservation.

As I assembled my notes and summoned my courage, I realized so much time had elapsed that I could rely on few primary sources—my parents had passed away decades earlier, and the family repository of letters had gone with the winds of time. Struggling to structure my story, I decided to build on personal memories, on those of my remaining siblings, and to some extent on those of the next generation The basic layout is a memoir of youth, though in places it is a family history, some legendary. Of necessity, I've taken liberties with my tale. In some instances I've created a narrative to flesh out a scene, but within parameters of known facts and history. On other occasions, I've invented dialogue which I hope reflects truthfully for a given character.

My writing was well underway as the federal elections of 2016 and 2018 came and went, and thoughtful people, I suspect, would murmur that a pattern of nationalism and anti-democracy has emerged. Because my story winds its way through the 1930s and 1940s, there is a need to consider those earlier years to reflect on the economic destabilization, the rising militarism and nationalism, and finally the all-out war that devastated much of the world. I hope this writing may illuminate some of the mistakes of our past and help place global peace uppermost in our hearts and minds.

CHAPTER 1

Down East, over Lubec, some hundred miles away, the sun had broken the horizon and had begun its relentless march westward across Maine. Its spears of light, nearly parallel to the earth, eventually glanced off my bedroom wall and gently aroused me. My sister Patsy, then a toddler, had wandered in during the night and lay like a family pet across the bottom of my cot. Not wanting to wake her, I drew up my knees, pitched out of bed, and stepped to the sun-filled window. I wanted to glimpse Gypsy Rock. I wanted to recount the events of the previous day and reassure myself that events had transpired as I remembered them.

Yesterday, late on a warm August afternoon, I had committed some transgression—or several—serious enough to elicit, "You're going to get it when your father gets home!" from my mother. My memory after all these decades leaves no clue as to which rule—or rules—of decorum I had breached. However, there appeared to be a certainty of punishment for bad behavior. An eight-year-old boy needn't question the admonition. And I didn't.

It was in late summer of 1939, though the first vestiges of autumn were noticeable and the days had been unusually warm—*dog days,* as we referred to them. Our home in Brewer, a modest-sized community on the banks of the Penobscot River, stood on a slight rise we called *the hilltop,* amidst a small cluster of clapboard houses and the Dougherty Brothers' dairy. A mile east of the river, the dairy farm with its pastures, barns, and haying fields was the most prominent feature of the landscape. Beyond the farm the land brushed up against woodlands and, with the exception of a few widely scattered farms and hamlets north and east of us, bordered the Maine woods, a vast sea of conifers, lakes, and wetlands extending to the Canadian border.

Having no plan, I raced out of the house and headed for the meadows and fields that stood across the way, green and inviting to a troubled youth. Within minutes—if I cared to look back—a screen of old apple trees and alders had separated me from home. I could have remained there in what was once a brickyard, with familiar hiding places where I'd successfully eluded playmates in the past. I could have amused myself there among the abandoned farm equipment, rusting "tin lizzies," and a Gothic-looking, deserted wooden fish house, its purpose now supplanted by modern refrigeration, sinking slowly back, back to the soil from which it came. But I needed distance; I needed separation!

A pronounced slope several times my height revealed the perimeters of the brickyard-cum-meadow. Approaching the incline, I could sense the presence of gangs of men generations ago, their pickaxes flashing in the sun, their shovels noisily clattering as they ripped out rich, gray scoops of clay, creating a rise in the terrain where the clay gave out and the digging ceased.

Shinnying up the bank, I heard fragments of loose dirt falling away behind me. When I gained the top, I looked homeward and could see the distant neighborhood rooftops. Ahead of me lay open haying fields, cut and gathered in recent weeks, now straw-colored in the late August sun. Farther away, in fields Mr. Dougherty had trimmed in late June, the grasses had rejuvenated and stood verdantly in contrast, awaiting a second cutting. A massive boulder we called Gypsy Rock rose in the midst of the farmland, a backdrop of birches and conifers which was Farrington's Woods profiling its gray-black eminence.

I hastily crossed the brown fields, happy that I'd been wearing my Keds sneakers—though at the end of summer the tops had started parting from the rubber soles—as the grass stalks were menacing to bare feet.

Reaching the rock, I halted briefly to catch my breath and to survey my proposed hiding place for the coming hours, or for who knew how long. An anomalous boulder, Gypsy Rock was as imposing as ever. It sat, dark and battleship-like, rising incongruously out of a sea of grasses. Likely a glacial erratic, it may have been ripped rudely from the hilly ledges of Clifton, a few miles north, and deposited here, as the mile-high glacier melted under it tens of thousands of years earlier. In my memory, it stood many times my height, higher than the brickyard slope I had just surmounted. (Viewing it more contemporaneously, it has shrunk but is still visible in the distant backyards of homes that now surround it.)

My siblings and I, along with neighborhood children, had visited the rock countless times and had warded off attackers in our versions of Capture the Flag. I wouldn't likely be fending off armies of attackers this day, but I needed possibly to feel secure and shielded from whatever might move in the night.

The irregularly shaped boulder measured some twenty-five to thirty feet along its base. I climbed to a familiar outcropping and proclaimed, Robinson Crusoe-like, my haven, an ideal crow's nest to observe the tempest that might be following me.

Suddenly overcome by fatigue, the emotions that had propelled me for the last hours having evaporated, I settled on a rocky slab that would oblige me as a bench and bed. I felt a contented warmth emanating from the stone beneath me, an assurance of comfort in the later hours.

I may have caused a disturbance at home, but here, as I observed the late afternoon breezes sweep across the fields, bending grasses like waves on a green sea, I was immersed in a domain of tranquility. Contrastingly— in the world beyond my youthful comprehension—war clouds had gathered above Central Europe (along the German–Polish border), and in England and on the Continent, people were holding their collective breaths. There would be but one more week of peace in that real world.

With darkness approaching and no visible life within a mile or two in any direction, an eight-year-old boy might have been considerably anxious, if not frightfully scared. I felt neither. Rather, I brought up my knees, adjusted my back against the warm stone, and pleasantly surveyed the diminishing day. To the west, directly in front of me and, through the fields and meadows looking homeward, the sky had taken on its first faint streaks of gold and red, promising a colorful sunset. I felt reassured of my actions, convinced I'd be sleeping under the stars and determined to stay my complacent course. Contentedly, I dozed off and allowed my mind to drift.

When I next gazed upward, it was decidedly more night than day. If we'd had a brilliant sunset, if we'd had an extended twilight, I'd missed them. Darkness now enveloped my world. Glancing toward the southeast, rather than homeward, I observed several intermittent, small flashes of light. I determined that those flickering lights could not be fireflies this late in the season. Must they have come from some other—nefarious—source? Had I possessed some club or stick, I would have grasped it more firmly. As it happened, I simply waited and watched anxiously.

The flashes continued their trajectory in my direction, their staggered nature indicating several unified sources. If it were a rescue party, it had definitely not come from home as I had. It appeared to have come from Eastern Avenue, which bordered the fields and to an extent demarked farmland from forest.

Gypsy Rock drew its name from a wandering and transient band of Gypsies that camped in the vicinity from time to time. I had viewed the tops of their tents and wagons only a year or two previously. They had inspired my curiosity, but my brother Bobby had warned me that they were a peculiar people who possessed an acquisitive behavior and were not to be trusted. For the most part, they kept to themselves and, like the winds, evanescently appeared and faded. I cautioned myself again that the lights could suggest Gypsies, and that I might have to abandon my rocky stronghold and flee into the nearby woods.

The flashes morphed into a steady beam of light. I could hear muffled voices. I felt a nervous but controlled excitability growing in my chest. A decision to abandon my perch seemed the prudent course. Suddenly, before I could gain my footing, a chorus of voices, growing in volume, chanted, "Paul, Paul, you can come home now!" And after a pause, "Mom is cooking your favorite, chicken 'n' dumplings!"

Their entreaty seemed sincere, and supper sounded enticing. I had made my youthful point!

The next morning, when my parents heard me arise, I was quietly summoned to their bedroom. I must have had some initial apprehension, and my misgivings were confirmed when I viewed their somber faces. Mother, speaking first, directed me to perform a series of errands in the neighborhood nearby and, later in the week, I was to accompany my oldest brother, Bobby, delivering his magazine route in Bangor, across the river. As she spoke, I noticed a crease had broken across my father's face, and a mischievous smile seemed forthcoming. When I was dismissed, my mother's countenance had softened as well.

By this time—1939—my parents had eight children, which would have put me somewhere in the middle. My parents' backgrounds were decidedly different. My mother had family with Eastern European roots, and she had been raised in metropolitan New York and nearby New Jersey. My father's family reached back to French Canada and possessed an additional heritage of Scots–Irish and rural Maine. They had met in New York City and, much against her family's wishes, married and, via steamship, moved off to Maine. They evidenced by all accounts a most agreeable marriage.

We had a large family, even by the standards of the first half of the twentieth century. After experiencing life in several residences in small-town Maine and later a little farm in Holden, my mother persuaded my dad to seek a permanent home in a more built-up environment, where children might walk to school and where grocery shopping needn't involve long-range planning.

In 1930, despite the crushing economic depression devastating the country, my father mustered up will and courage and purchased a modest parcel of land on the outskirts of Brewer. The land, bordering a large tract of fields owned by the Holyoke family and across the street from the Doughertys' farm, was a pleasant half acre. Together with his father, Alexandre (my grandfather), a retired master carpenter, they initiated construction of a wood-framed story-and-a-half bungalow on the front of the lot. It was well crafted with pronounced eaves, beautiful brackets, and generous roof overhangs that flared upward.

Meanwhile, the economy had worsened, with unemployment rampant, the banking system in chaos, and a president, Herbert Hoover, unable or unwilling to take any major corrective actions. Few families could escape its effects and certainly not my parents. Consequently, after partitioning most of the house, they elected to delay finishing the interior and move in. The landscaping and surrounding picket fence would wait several years to be realized. Nevertheless, little No. 159 would be the pride and envy of Chamberlain Street. It was most timely for my mother, who was heavy with her fifth child (*moi*!).

As I descended the stairs, I realized I had been dealt my punishment. I had passed over some invisible threshold of maturity, as well. Henceforth, I'd be treated more as a young adult and less as a child. My chastisement contained elements of family harmony: Care and cohesiveness of family were as valued as law and order.

As I reached the kitchen, the faint odor of hot oatmeal warming on the stove greeted me. Several of my siblings were gathered at the table, and I joined them. Their eyes could not conceal their quiet envy (or glee) that I had misbehaved but had escaped major retribution. I decided not to gloat or boast about my adventure. I just ate my Quaker Oats without comment.

Mother appeared in the kitchen nearly as soon as I. It was evident she had been down in the early hours and had commenced her morning rituals of producing freshly brewed coffee and preparing our cereal. Her kitchen, spare but adequate, contained a glossy cream-and green-enameled Glenwood stove piped to an exposed brick chimney. Originally wood-fired, it was presently fueled by kerosene. In those days, the stove was the focal point of most kitchens. Next to it, in an elegant oak cabinet, stood the icebox, cooled by fifty-pound blocks of ice. A cupboard on which much of the food for the table was prepared occupied an opposite wall. It was a utilitarian—and sometimes the only—cabinet in rural kitchens. On the same wall, under large double-hung windows, a gleaming white sink resided, a gingham skirt prettily disguising what lay below. Complementing the kitchen were numerous open shelves for dishes and cookware. Our kitchen no doubt reflected the times, though possibly a step down for my mother, whose homes in a metropolitan area would have featured natural gas piped in from the street and many other conveniences. She never complained.

Seeing that I'd finished my breakfast, Mom spooned up the remnants of the oatmeal and placed them in front of me. I knew the drill: I was to deliver the cereal to the Fords across the field and return home with a copy of yesterday's *Bangor Daily News*. It was a long-standing swapping arrangement struck between our families, wherein the leftovers were for the Fords' chickens (Mother always cooked an abundance), and we received a day-old newspaper. It hardly mattered that we returned with yesterday's news. It seemed events came about more slowly in those days, and anyway the radio with its noontime, six-, and nine-o'clock news was more immediate.

Swapping and trading were common in that time. The process allowed for a friendlier neighborhood, presenting an opportunity to validate the appreciation and respect we held for each other. A few years later, I would end my newspaper delivery route at the Doughertys' farm, where I would give Mr. Dougherty the day's newspaper, and he would hand me a half pint of chocolate milk, a tasty layer of rich cream visible below the cap.

I never considered going to the Fords anything but an agreeable task. Besides the paper, Mrs. Ford, a kindly, plump woman in her eighties, her hair positioned in a bun above a smiling face, would usually reward us with a gingerbread cookie, still warm from her wood-burning oven. The cookie, which reportedly had its origin in the lumber camps of the Maine woods, was an unforgettable confection. Larger than my small hand and soft inside (never brittle), they were finished with a light powdered sugar dusting. In essence they were more cake than cookie. Though the errand was my specific duty this week, we often argued as to who would obtain the mission with its sweet ending.

With thoughts of my escapade well behind me, I set out in the late morning, as my mother had directed me, to visit Miss Farrington who lived down below us on Chamberlain Street. Alice Farrington, now elderly, was the niece of Joshua Chamberlain, whose gallant stand at Little Round Top in the battle of Gettysburg made him an icon for bravery in the Civil War, and for whom our street was named. He went on to an illustrious career as president of Bowdoin College and governor of Maine.

Miss Farrington lived in a most attractive Greek Revival house, white with green shutters, at the intersection of Washington and Chamberlain Streets. As I approached her house, a granite hitching post and an elevated stone stoop with its wrought iron boot scraper spoke of an earlier time, when her callers arrived in fancy horse-drawn carriages. The front entrance was there at the gable end, but I reasoned my inelegant and unannounced arrival would be more successful at the rear door. Progressing to the rear porch, I prayed she wouldn't see me, though I had to pass her study in the handsome windowed ell along the side.

I rapped on the door and waited. A feeling of not relishing the task crept over me, and with good reason. Scary stories about Miss Farrington abounded. She could inspire both fear and awe in children. I had viewed her chiefly from a distance and now anticipated a face-to-face meeting with trepidation. After I'd waited several anxious moments, she answered my knock and, eyeing me carefully, invited me in. I could feel her gaze as I simultaneously studied her. Bespectacled, with tiny steel-rimmed glasses accentuating a frail but intent face, Alice Farrington stood firmly in front of me in a drab brown woolen dress topped by a heavy shawl draping down to her ankles, despite the heat. I had seen that same musty vision peering out of the old photographs, ones marking the going off to war of fathers, sons, and husbands and the somber women they were leaving behind. She sensed my mission before I could fully enunciate it.

Lorraine, our oldest sibling, worked intermittently for Miss Farrington, and no doubt Alice Farrington acknowledged me as one of the Landry boys. I was aware too, from their working arrangement, that Miss Farrington was an exacting employer. While Lorraine was supposed to be—as I overheard my mother say—some sort of girl Friday, Alice Farrington treated her as a youthful scrub lady. My sister commonly frowned whenever she discussed the old woman.

Miss Farrington suggested I wait in the kitchen whilst she rummaged for an envelope in the study. She added that I was welcome to step into the front hall when she noticed me peeking in that direction. The agile old lady wheeled around and, with alacrity, left me. I watched her diminutive but formidable figure, hair neatly braided behind her, disappear into the study.

The pieces of my errand were adding up: My sister needed money owed to her, but she didn't intend to continue the abusive relationship. I understood Lorraine's distaste for the niece of Joshua Chamberlain, but this woman, her house, and her connection to Governor Chamberlain nevertheless fascinated me. I glanced around the hall as I waited. The space was replete with ancient photographs, one long, horizontal image being that of the 20th Maine Regiment, her uncle's command, before it left the state for the South in the early 1860s. Alice's cat, a fluffy overweight feline, brushed by me as I inspected the photos. The cat paid me little more attention than did Alice.

Taking a few steps, I easily viewed several Victorian upholstered parlors and a formal dining room adorned with antique photographs of the ruins of Rome and Athens. The rooms were dimly illuminated, even in midday, the green shades pulled down, drapes drawn close, a Boston fern sitting timelessly on the hearth. The whole was enveloped with a stale but not unpleasant odor of wood smoke, cats, and old carpets. Somewhere, a clock issued a muffled tolling of the hour. Time, I intuited, moved slowly in this house.

Strolling back to the kitchen, I heard drawers closing, confirming that Miss Farrington had finished her search. I took a last look into the pantry and scullery where Lorraine had labored but would not revisit. I wished to linger, but I could hear the lady of the house returning. As I stood, one hand on the doorknob, she handed me a well-used envelope, saying, "Give this to your sister. Good-bye."

Traipsing leisurely back up the hill, I recounted that I'd accomplished my task diplomatically and promptly and...I had survived Alice Farrington!

A few days later, after my success with Miss Farrington, my brother Bobby came to fetch me as I was playing with several friends. I was to help him with his magazine deliveries in Bangor after lunch. I must have exhibited some initial reluctance to forsake my playmates, which forced Bobby to remind me that this was part of the deal with my parents. It was a seminal reminder: I was being yanked, gently but firmly, from my childish world and nudged into an adult's realm of work and responsibility.

For both financial and family purposes, there existed an encouragement to contribute, to share the burden. Among my siblings, our industriousness was displayed in numerous venues: newspaper and magazine delivery routes, gathering empty soda bottles (occasionally lifted from other neighborhoods) and collecting a two-cent deposit, and selling candy bars. A box of twelve cost a dollar and was sold at ten cents per bar, a gross profit of twenty cents. (These sales were often to our magazine customers, an economy of marketing!). The older children might also engage in snow shoveling or lawn mowing, as well as working after school or weekends at a local farm or grocery store. The general rule observed was that a portion of our earnings was given to the family. I never resented paying my share because I received abundant care and love in return. We were, after all, a family!

We prepared lunch that noon, sitting around the kitchen table. The radio was blaring a scarcely tolerable cowboy tune by a group of western singers and string instrumentalists under the moniker of "Jimmy and Dick." A small ensemble of husbands and wives, they had drifted across the country from North Dakota and taken root in our area. They weren't particularly good musicians—their Western twang collided with our New England ears—and they weren't truly cowboys. But they were popular with Maine folk, enduring for years. My next oldest brother, Junior (George, Jr.), would attempt at times to acquire another station and "real music," whereupon a heated commotion would ensue.

The older siblings were exceedingly muscular young men. Contrastingly, my brothers Floyd and Hutch (Howard) and I shared more modest physiques, though we would eventually better them in height. If the older siblings squared off, it was Bobby who would prevail. Today, it would be "Jimmy and Dick!"

Lunch finished, Bobby grabbed a cloth newspaper delivery sack from the shed enclosing the rear steps, under which all manner of shoes, boots, rubbers, and skates were stored. He motioned for me to join him. We hiked across our backyard, cutting angularly through neighbors' fields, and reached a steep ridge and gully that would deliver us out to State Street. I was familiar with this path, as it comprised a shortcut to Kelliher's Market. The store was a convenient source for last-minute ingredients essential for dinner, as well as a place to redeem those two-cent deposits for bottles we'd gathered. It stood directly opposite Brewer High School and it cheerfully fed the sweet tooth of a generation of students. We didn't possess the craving or the time to visit Kelliher's this day.

Bobby and I followed State Street, heading to the bridge, chatting as we walked. State Street was a most attractive thoroughfare, lined with a procession of American elm trees and venerable maples. Called the Bar Harbor Road by some, it had recently been paved with concrete, its sidewalks meeting manicured lawns on either side. Bobby, as he was called until he graduated from high school, seemed to know everyone. He informed me as to who lived where, who the parents were—if they owned a business or had a profession—and if the sons were athletic or the daughters good-looking. People would hail him readily. I liked being in Bobby's company. He always appeared confident and in charge. He also knew how to protect himself with his fists—and you, too, if you were with him.

A year or two earlier, I'd had difficulty dropping off something for my mom at a neighbor's house farther out Chamberlain Street. The family employed a large, hostile watchdog, as they lived in a relatively remote part of the street and were frequently absent. Each time I advanced toward the door, the dog would viciously challenge me. I was not afraid of animals, but the savageness of this animal set me to tears. I returned home dejectedly, having failed at completing my task. At that point, Bobby offered to return with me and help complete my mission. When the canine again came at us, Bobby stoically held his ground—me behind him—and when the dog lunged, its nose met Bobby's fist. The blow tumbled the animal and set it howling to its backyard, licking its wounds. My brother later informed me it had *not* been a lucky punch. Rather it had been a calculated blow aimed at the soft spot above the dog's ferocious jaws and timed to land when the creature was most vulnerable. Brother Bobby was my protector, and whether I understood his clever maneuver I don't remember.

The bridge over the Penobscot River to Bangor was a demarcation separating the modest small town of Brewer from its robust and bustling big cousin, Bangor. On the Brewer side, huddled around Penobscot Square, stood a few businesses like Mack Baking Company, Dodge's Market, and Burr's Drug Store. A Central Maine Railroad crossing, with its small shack and pipe-smoking watchman, penetrated the square and caused occasional traffic backups, as trains proceeded east to the rail terminus near Ellsworth. We waved to the watchman as we advanced to the bridge's entrance. We also waved to Mr. Burr. Alfonse Burr not only dispensed medicines and remedies, but cheerfully offered advice on everything from sports to politics to how parents should discipline their children.

Crossing the planking that formed the bridge's sidewalk, we encountered a highly audible buzz and constant vibration as automobiles drove steadily across the steel-girded structure. Below us, tidewaters raced between the Bangor Hydro dam above and the ocean's entrance to Penobscot River fifty miles downstream. Tides frequently exceeded four feet here with their attendant swift and swirling waters, yet that did little to discourage youngsters who lived on adjacent streets from climbing on the bridge and plunging into the dangerous whirlpools twenty feet below. We passed a dozen or more boys, their hair and tanned bodies dripping rivulets, laughingly waiting their turn to drop out of sight. They loved bantering with the passersby as they clung, defiantly, to the outside of the metal-braced railings.

The two towns have always embraced the river. The headwaters of the Penobscot lie to the north, in the upper reaches of Moosehead Lake and the vast lake country north and east of that region, The river possesses many moods as it cascades and twists, tumbles and flows to its destiny—the Atlantic. In places it is broad and still, deceptively so, with treacherous currents lurking beneath. In other places it is exuberant and impetuous, exhibiting raw energy that, if tamed, can power industry. When those waters are malevolent, however, they can sweep away the inattentive to their doom.

A stern warning existed in our home; no playing or swimming in the waters of Penobscot River!

The bridge and its sidewalk arched over several railroad tracks before ending. Often locomotives pulling and switching rail traffic would pass underneath, sending aloft clouds of steam and smoke and charging the air with excitement. We ended up on Bangor's Washington Street, at that time a wide expanse of cobblestone. An occasional team of horses, plodding noisily to some back alley, could still be observed here and nearby, with cars and delivery trucks lined impatiently behind them. Here we entered the magazine distributor's place of business, our first destination.

Bobby introduced me to the owner and his son. I was already acquainted with the younger man, as he'd been keen on my sister Lorraine and would sometimes drop off comic books for the enjoyment of the more junior children. (I'm not sure his efforts curried any special favor from my sister.) We picked up several dozen copies of *Liberty* magazine that then, like *Collier* and *The Saturday Evening Post*, was a popular periodical. A second bag was procured for me, and we loaded our wares. My sack fell well below my knees as we headed out to the street.

Washington Street hummed with vitality. There was a stream of activity in and around Union Station, a yellow brick edifice poised romantically but solidly anchoring the street. The cacophony of locomotives gushing steam, steel wheels shrieking on the steel rails, and the multitude of voices rising resounded like a Bartok symphony. In one direction, the stir and movement lingered a short distance to a span dubbed "the Tin Bridge" crossing the Kenduskeag Stream, which emptied into the Penobscot nearby. It was but a short walk away from the point where the *Bonton,* a now discontinued ferry, had disembarked its passengers from across the river. In the other direction, where we walked, the din persisted along Exchange Street, and on sunny days dozens of unemployed and disheveled woodsmen sat propped up against storefronts, sleeping off an alcohol-induced haze. Bobby stated that "these poor devils" subsisted in flophouses and cheap bars and eating establishments, slowly exhausting their meager savings. When their money was gone, he added, they would sometimes consume vanilla extract or breathe canned heat (used to warm chafing dishes and often purloined) to achieve an intoxicated high. "If they survive till fall," he lamented, "they might return to the woods."

As we navigated through the sidewalks of crouching humanity, Bobby sounded a note of caution, "They're dirty but harmless." I wasn't to speak to or otherwise engage them. My big brother held my hand securely as we made our way through Bangor's version of the Bowery. It was disheartening for me to witness these grown men slowly wasting away in public view. Somehow though, the seaminess of the street didn't spoil the ambience and the exhilarating image I was shaping of the city.

I struggled to keep up with Bobby as we neared our first delivery, on the fourth floor of an office building. It was located at one of Bangor's busiest intersections, Exchange and State Streets, and a policeman was urging reluctant motorists to proceed or turn without blocking traffic. We walked through the lobby shared with a drug store and ascended the stairs. My bag was chafing my legs, and the temperature was rising as we steadily climbed. Battling with my load, I was determined to be "Mr. Businessman," a self-employed, novice entrepreneur. There was no elevator, largely true throughout commercial buildings in town. Reaching our designated floor, we could hear the steady clatter of typewriters amid the volubility of human voices competing with fans struggling to provoke a breeze. Adding to the buzz was a dissonance welling up from the street. It was a noisy but inviting atmosphere. We dropped off our *Liberty* magazine at several desks, received payment (usually including a tip), and descended to the second floor. We walked into a dental lab, where a dozen moldings sat on shelves waiting to be replicated into false teeth, and nodded to the technician. He watched casually, thanked us, and without taking his hands off the plaster of Paris, told us to take money from a small dish by the entrance. We did so, but we didn't take or even consider a gratuity.

We continued our rounds, dropping off our publications at various locations: the Merrill Trust Company, as well as several other banks, H. B. Dunning Company, sundry doctors and lawyers, and Mr. Pooler's Lighthouse Loans, where folks who didn't qualify for a bank loan might seek alternative financing. (Though never discussing their own finances, our parents talked frequently about such matters at the dinner table.) Mr. Pooler was a good, church-going man and I presumed he did well for his clients. His office was beautifully updated in a 1930s contemporary style with glass-block walls and clean-lined furniture, all of which was more interesting to me than financing.

As our loads lessened, I was no longer struggling. We trudged up Main Street just as the *Bangor Daily Commercial* paper hit the street. Young energetic voices, more suggestive of choirboys than street hawkers, were touting the headlines of the day, adding, "Read all about it!" The news of the day reverberated in our ears as we crossed the city's busy main shopping street and headed for Freese's Department Store, where we gained entrance through a throng of perspiring people.

The fans were spinning away here, too, and clearly in a losing battle. The soda fountain stood just off the entry, with its polished green-and-black granite, looking cool and welcoming. The classic chrome-upholstered bar stools and the bent-iron ice cream chairs and tables were most beckoning. Alas, there was no room for two more! My brother seemed not dismayed.

We recrossed Main Street and entered Frawley's, where the jukebox and raucous but gay voices greeted us. Bobby was momentarily lost in a crowd of friends and acquaintances. This was hardly a difficult choice, I thought, as several young people offered us a place at their table. I received a double scoop of coffee ice cream ("How 'bout hot fudge on top?") for my endeavors. I felt both successful and well paid.

Having finished our route, we walked above Freese's, turned down a side street, passing the Olympia Theatre, and entered another of Bangor's distinctive squares. In New England, a square existed wherever significant streets intersected and commercial businesses and community activities gathered and thrived. It became a common and simplified definition of a neighborhood. Bobby readily and colorfully etched some history of Pickering Square as we strolled through. It was a relic of Bangor's rambunctious, lumbering past. Like Exchange Street, a great number of bars still existed, but the derelicts were much fewer in evidence. The square was discovering new life with a mixed crowd. There appeared to be well-dressed businessmen and exuberant male college students. As Bob related euphemistically, the area had been a place "for a man to dodge prohibition and slake his thirst." (Again, we'd talked about those things at the dinner table, but had observed little alcohol consumption on my parents' part other than an occasional friendly gathering with joyful voices celebrating a birthday or New Year's Eve. We youngsters sometimes watched the merrymaking furtively from the stairway.) The square still held a number of wood-planked sidewalks, such as you might see in Western movies, and numerous dirt side streets and alleys. I could feel—and even hear—the rhythms of the past as we strode over the boards. I could envision burly lumberjacks eying a little libation to celebrate the end of a day or a season of arduous—and frequently dangerous—work in the woods, on the river, and in the sawmills. Add to that the sailors off the coastal schooners and the shipbuilders and the brickmakers across the river in Brewer. It must have been simultaneously hellish and compelling. In some ways it still was.

It's convenient sometimes to consider towns existing on either side of the river as "twin cities." While Bangor and Brewer shared much more than they diverged, the differences in my time were notable. Bangor, the larger of the two by far, was heavily Irish Catholic and tended to vote for progressive Democrats. In contrast, Brewer was more Protestant, conservative, and seemingly more Yankee, favoring the Republican ticket through the Depression and war years. While Bangor had a lively and thriving downtown—which we'd just visited—Brewer's commercial district was comprised of but a few blocks of stores clustered by the bridge.

Bangor exuded an openness, a welcoming hand to all ethnicities: a prosperous Jewish community, with its synagogue and Sklar's Delicatessen, which would make a New Yorker (such as my mother) proud; Greek families with their restaurants and businesses; and a sprinkling of Chinese and Filipinos. Contrastingly, the city fathers of Brewer had authorized, and the townspeople had cheered, a parade of the Ku Klux Klan in 1924. (Some years later, my younger brother and I would discover a cache of KKK literature still in an attic of the building where my family's business was located. The boxes were replete with anti-immigration, anti-black, and anti-Catholic bigotry.)

By the time of my youth, whatever antagonisms existed were settled good naturedly, but enthusiastically, on the playing field each November 11th—Armistice Day, celebrating the end of hostilities in the First World War—and at other times in the scholastic year.

My family's future appeared bright that fall, and I looked forward to seeing old school chums in the weeks ahead. The plans to finish the construction of our home, particularly completing the interior of the house, stirred my interest.

Father frequently asked me to help him on a weekend, when he'd take up a project. I was both pleased and proud to be engaged, especially if the work involved carpentry or some creative skill. He would even request my opinion of something as we worked side-by-side building a bookcase or constructing screens for the shed. His knowledge of woodworking, gained from my grandfather, seemed endless. His views of a complex world were impressive as well—he could explain, for my comprehension, the aurora borealis (about which I'd asked) or Russian Bolshevism (about which I'd not asked) with equanimity and precision. I found myself really seeing my father for the first time. I needed to discover this man, not solely as a parent, but for the intricate, multifaceted individual he was. Likewise, I needed to learn about my mother, and of the paths that had brought them together.

CHAPTER 2

My dad, born in 1901, was the son and only child of Alexandre Landry and Hannah Liscomb. Alex, as most people knew him, was from Tracadie, a small town in New Brunswick, Canada. The Landry clan was part of an enforced migration of French Acadians expelled from Nova Scotia over a century earlier by the British, as France and England struggled for dominance in the New World.

A modest young man, Alexandre grew up in a family that prized its culture, music, and wood artisanship, embracing the Catholic Church and its connections to faraway Brittany. It was an isolated life of forest and sea on the eastern edge of Maritime Canada, but compensated by a closeness of family, community, and faith. The woods and nearby bays provided a living that sustained the people well in the pleasant months. The winter months, however, were depressingly bleak; unemployment was universal, money and food scarce.

Alex, over thirty and with hopes of steady work and a better future, traveled overland and crossed the border into Maine. There he joined hundreds of other Canadian men in cutting down immense virgin pines, hauling and floating them down Maine's swiftly flowing rivers, and sawing the huge-diameter logs into acceptable dimensions for the hungry lumber markets of Boston, New York, and beyond. It was an industry that, contrary to Alex's native New Brunswick, went nearly full bore in the winter and had a pronounced slackness in the summer. Speaking little or no English, he often returned home to Tracadie in the good weather.

Hannah Elizabeth Liscomb, daughter of Scots and Irish parents, was born and brought up in Hampden, a charming small town on the western bank of the Penobscot, below Bangor. The river waters were navigable for deep-keeled vessels at least to the vicinity of Hampden, and it was, like nearby Winterport, an anchorage for retired sea captains. Lizzie, as her friends called her, was schooled at Hampden Academy, which admitted young ladies, unusual for that time. She found her calling as a midwife. There were few if any obstetricians in Eastern Maine in the late nineteenth century, and the assistance of a midwife was the norm for many expectant mothers. A midwife might work alone or in company with a physician, in what was largely an itinerant profession. Her services could range from childbirth to pre- and postnatal care. Hannah Liscomb, her blond hair tied up in an attractively ribboned bun could frequently be observed riding in a carriage driven by one of Bangor's prominent doctors, like Dr. Bunting, on an urgent mission. Her penchant for her work hadn't allowed time for children and family of her own, but her love of children inspired her then and later to foster little ones, if the mother died or the family couldn't care for another child.

After several seasons in the Maine woods, Alex Landry worked his way down the west branch of the Penobscot River and found himself in Bangor. It may have been at a friend's celebration for a newborn, or it may have been just a serendipitous moment. Whatever the event, Alex met Lizzie. While the two could hardly have shared much in common—neither could fluently speak the other's language—they apparently hit it off. Perhaps it was his stout but taut body, his handsome tanned face with its large unclipped mustache. What she wouldn't have failed to notice was his *joie de vivre*, his immoderate smile. Alex saw a beguiling face, large blue eyes, and blond hair artfully bound up, but now attractively tousled by the wind. She didn't suggest a lithe feminine creature, though her moderate weight was conceivably alluring if not seductive at the turn of the century. Both had passed the forty-year mark. Finding their new friendship mutually satisfying, they married.

Little Georgie, my father, was born a year or two later. The new parents were elated. The village of Tracadie in New Brunswick was overjoyed.

Alex and Lizzie, taking their newborn with them, moved to a small farm in Corinth, on the northeastern outskirts of Bangor, where Alex had constructed a new home. The house was similar to those throughout Eastern—and particularly French-speaking—Canada. A story-and-a-half cottage, its large wood-shingled roof pitched steeply toward the road and curved artfully over an open porch. Fireplaces had died out of favor, but there were several wood stoves that provided warmth and ambience to the snug little farmhouse. The whole family slept downstairs at first, though when little Georgie was four or five, he was given his own bedroom upstairs under the eaves.

Alexandre Landry—woodcarver, musician (violin), and master carpenter—was determined to have a small but adequate barn as well. He therefore built a moderate structure that would shelter a milking cow or two, a woodworking shop, and an ell with a ten-foot high entrance for keeping a horse. Little Georgie, after his parents allowed him his own space in the cottage, could wake in the morning and watch General, the family's draft animal, amble in and out of his stable. A moderately built stallion, General was used for multiple purposes around the farm and, because their son had no close playmates, he became Georgie's companion. Georgie loved recalling how the animal, even in a blinding blizzard, could be told, "Go home, General!" and the horse would follow a precise route, without command, to the barn, from any distance.

While Momma Hannah homeschooled their child (nobody called it homeschooling at that time) in his reading and writing, she instilled in him good Protestant morals. Georgie was reading at an early age, his books outnumbering his toys under the eaves. Alex frequently brought him out to the shop to learn the rudiments and love of woodworking. Constructing a home and its outbuildings left a beneficial residue of wood pieces, of all sorts and dimensions. It provided a candy store of opportunities to build useful things for the farm and to both delight and educate his son. He showed his boy the small violin he'd carved and assembled when he was a youth. He had carried the instrument with him over the years and miles since leaving New Brunswick. Georgie beamed with admiration as his fingers felt the violin's strings and sensed its well-proportioned curves.

Alex went to a corner of the shop where he stored a large toolbox and pulled out an assemblage of chisels and gouges. With these tools, along with a pocket knife, he set his son to work at the bench carving blocks of soft pine into recognizable shapes. He taught the young lad to recognize and work with the grain—and sometimes against the grain—to achieve the desired outcome. In time, Georgie would move on to the larger tools and more ambitious projects, all the while reveling in a new world where art and craftsmanship met in a scrap of wood.

Life on their small farm in Corinth, when time to be with wife and child presented itself, was a special joy for Alexander. As a master carpenter, his main livelihood, more often than not, involved constructing large homes or commercial structures several days journey from the farm. Typically, he would gather a small crew, travel by wagon and train to somewhere on the coast of Maine below Portland, and build one of the numerous fine resort hotels overlooking the shore. In those days, the first decades of the 1900s, a master carpenter was viewed as a general contractor, sometimes as the architect as well, who could lay out the foundation following a building plan—whether his or a bona fide architect's—and bring the edifice to completion and acceptance by the owner. Beyond the framing of these structures, many finished externally in the so-called "shingle style," every surface of roof and wall was graced with aromatic cedar shingles. Others, in the Queen Anne style, contained open but covered porches, turrets, dormers, and recesses that expressed an age of elegance and freedom of design, again with an abundance of shingled sheathing. Many of these eminent wooden structures would survive for a century. (A few are still with us in Kennebunk Beach, and elsewhere on the coast and in the mountains.)

When Georgie reached the age of about eleven, having exceeded Hannah's ability to confidently instruct him, and there being no public school beyond sixth grade available to him, Alex decided to take his son that spring to his job site in Southern Maine. The boy, of course, was enraptured, his mother downcast, as father and son rolled the heavy green tool chest across the shop floor and slid it on to the wagon. Hannah had known the time was coming when a preadolescent would want to take his road to manhood, but could hardly accept that this was the moment. The three of them hugged, kissed, and cried soft tears, as Georgie, his blond hair stirring in the March breezes, his shoulders nearly as high as his dad's, jumped into the back of the neighbor's carriage for the ride to the train station. When the carriage dipped out of sight a few hundred yards away, Hannah, her cheeks still wet, reflected that this had always been the way for young boys in the country. Her consolation was, happily, he'd be with his father. For the next several months she'd be busy with farm chores, caring for a considerable garden, and watching for the postal stage and its letters from husband and son.

Through a long spring of alternating snow showers and warming sun, Georgie watched teams of horses clearing the grounds, and later scooping the earth away to prepare for a foundation. Each day thereafter, for weeks, teams would arrive with huge granite slabs to build the foundation wall. Once the walls were built up to the surface of the surrounding soil, masons were employed, using brick or smaller stones, to finish the walls another two or three feet to accommodate the broad sills that would hold the building's frame and wed it to its base. Eyeing the structure taking shape, the boy would emulate the carpenter's cutting and nailing the framework together; at other times he'd whittle away at selected scraps the workers would toss to him. He seemed never to be bored.

On Sunday all work would cease. Some but not all of the crew would attend church. Alex would faithfully go to Sunday Mass as he would throughout his life. He would usually offer to take his son. Georgie, however, would never feel the compulsion to go off, without breakfast, to receive the Eucharist; he'd rather play with his pocketknife among the wooden scraps and shingles. If he did accompany his dad, he might be accorded a special Sunday lunch at a tavern or eating place in the village. They would likely take an excursion by wagon or trolley as well, to see a local site or attraction. He'd be given a penny or two to buy a postcard, usually depicting what he'd viewed, which he'd excitedly write to his mother. After several years, at differing places, Alex would allow his son to amble on his own and explore whatever the town offered. He frequently would end up on the town wharf, mesmerized by the movement of both wind- and steam-powered vessels. This would set the lad to dreaming of places and events far from the coastal villages of Maine.

One Sunday, father and son traveled up to Portland where they joined hundreds of others welcoming two US Navy destroyers that lay anchored in Casco Bay. Launches, loaded with sailors anxious for a few hours on shore, were disembarking just as Georgie and his father arrived. The lad was favorably struck by the seamen, attired uniformly in white blouses, their collars catching the salty breeze and hats pulled jauntily down, just above their eyes. The launches that had brought the sailors to shore for liberty offered the citizens of Portland a ride out to the vessels. Alex and Georgie accepted the opportunity and rode out with about twenty others. The cruise out to the ships could not, because of the crowds involved and the limited space aboard the vessels, allow passengers to board. They were entranced however as the launch circled the small fleet of ships with four-stacked funnels, their gray hulls and identity numerals glistening with fresh paint, their gun turrets smartly aligned, and decorative signal flags snapping in the wind. The boy felt an emotion he couldn't fully fathom. His life, he sensed, was being pushed on a new tack. Alex silently acknowledged something about his son, too, though he hoped he was wrong.

By spring of 1918, the nation had been at war with Germany almost a year. Young men were being called up and going off to training camps. About four million men would serve in the country's armed services. Over two million Americans were to be transported to France. To the Navy would fall the task of bringing the American Expeditionary Force to Europe, safely and in large enough numbers to assure a turning of the tide in the long-stagnated Western Front. A secondary job, but essential to the success of the first order, was to assist our British allies in controlling the seas. This necessitated an enlarged navy equipped for anti-submarine and escort purposes. Georgie was determined to do his part, A pride of patriotism welled in Georgie's upper body, a spirit that a thousand pledges of allegiance could not bestow. Almost overnight, Georgie became George.

Now a strapping sixteen-year-old, George exceeded his father in height by half a foot, and his Sunday clothes no longer fit his growing frame. He sat down with his parents after supper one evening to inform them of his plan to join the Navy. There was a momentary silence on the part of all, but the disappointment on his parents' faces was unmistakable. Youngsters from Maine had a long history of "going down to the sea in ships." Youths, sometimes no older than twelve, escaping a cruel life at home or in company with an older relative or close friend who'd teach and care for them, would ship out to return years later as young men. George shared none of these reasons; he was driven by patriotism and a burning desire for adventure. Because he was following a path that was not unusual for Maine youth, nobody at home questioned his age.

A few days later, George kissed his mother farewell, harnessed up General to the family buggy, and, with his dad driving, headed down to Bangor and an exciting and unpredictable future. As news travels quickly and mysteriously in the country, several adjacent farmers and their wives and youngsters appeared waving to Alex and his son as they drove by. George tried to hold back his fears of separating from family and the only home he'd ever known. The two talked little on their slow trot to town, letting the sounds of General's plodding hooves fill the vacuum. As they neared their drop-off point, near City Hall, the young man began talking glibly about everything he'd repressed during the brief trip, his appreciation for the time father and son had spent closely working and exploring together. The young man alighted from the carriage with little baggage other than his shaving kit and an extra clean shirt. His dad sat motionless, holding the reins and trying to affect a smile. Professing his love for his parents, George stood on the curb and bear hugged his father. Yes, he'd write as frequently as he could and added, "Tell Momma I love her."

The torch was passing from the parents to the United States Navy. As he strode to the recruiting office and his swearing-in, a large poster proclaimed, "Uncle Sam Wants You!"

The train, referred to as Maine Central Railroad's milk train, moved slowly that morning through Northern Maine Junction, Benton and dozens of other small towns where, indeed, milk rather than passengers was the common commodity. George, though a well-built, muscular youngster, had yet to achieve his full growth. He'd eaten without appetite early that morning but now could feel an intense hunger. When the "Armstrong" peddler came by his seat, he purchased a not-so-fresh-looking apple with one of his few coins and sat back contentedly munching and reading the *Bangor Daily News.*

In Portland, a short layover would occur where he would transfer to a Boston & Maine car for the balance of the trip. A number of new passengers, mail and baggage cars, and, to his delight, a cheerfully lighted dining car, would join the train. A score of young men, not unlike himself, accompanied him as he shuffled down the aisle seeking an assigned seat. He quickly learned that many of these men, from every corner of the state, would be fellow recruits at the Boston Navy Yard.

George, who made friends readily, immediately set to chatting with his new companions, all on the same mission. Their fresh faces suggested they might be of an age; their rugged looks hinted of pushing forks full of hay high overhead and rowing out to fishing grounds out of sight of land and pulling in heavy nets. Still talking, they entered the dining car, its elegantly decorated interior startling to many of the sons of farmers and fishermen. George, having experienced refined dining in the hotels his father had built and from lessons Hannah had imparted to her son, carefully (but not *too* gracefully) selected the right fork and placed his napkin properly. They continued their animated conversations as the dining car manager collected their government-issued vouchers, and George noted the uniformly brown, well-calloused hands they—and he— exhibited. He admired his new buddies, his soon-to-be comrades in arms.

Sometime after the train had crossed the state border at Portsmouth, George realized he'd never traveled out of Maine. Maine had been his world for sixteen years, and now he'd be seeing those places older folks had mentioned—Boston and beyond. After the train glided across the Merrimack River, the conductor, making his rounds, alerted the young men that a representative of the Navy would be meeting them at a partic- ular spot in the station in about an hour's time. George reclined in his seat, quietly reflecting on what was to come and dozed off, as others had. He woke as the vibration under the car changed in pitch and the brakemen up forward slowed the train for its entry into Boston's North Station.

The recruits walked for about a hundred yards outside along the cars they had ridden in, before they encountered a bos'n (boatswain) 2nd class who'd gather and transport them to the basic training facility at the Boston Navy Yard. Noticeably absent was the solicitude of the recruiting team in Bangor. As drill instructors and their staffs have done before and will after, the bos'n shook his head in body language that could only indicate disap- proval of his newly acquired charges. He spoke clearly but gruffly to the recruits, referencing them as "lads" and "boys." They formed two lines and, as he barked orders, marched awkwardly out of the station and mounted the motorized vehicle that would carry them to South Boston. On the trip to the base, the lads looked at each other, not with fear or apprehension, but with acknowledgement that this is the Navy!

At five thirty the next morning—it was midweek—"Boats," as the Navy affectionately called its bos'ns, noisily rattled a large galvanized can that could conceivably be heard throughout the base. "Boys," Bos'n Mate James Moran informed them, "We have a very busy day, and a short week." They stumbled and ambled along to the base barber shop where barbers, smiling devilishly, subjected them to regulation haircuts, moderately long on the top, severely short on the sides and back. They next marched to the supply shed where each recruit received a batch of uniforms (blue and white blouses and pants), the dress blue pants having thirteen buttons in front and laced in the back, and a quantity of shoes and socks and skivvies, along with hats, gloves, and peacoat, all placed ultimately in a new seabag with their names stenciled thereon. Thus laden, they marched back to their barracks to "shower and get dressed in your undress blues." To most of the recruits, the shower was a totally new experience. In the background, Boats sounded out, "I want you nice and clean and shampooed; you've got ten minutes!" The balance of the day and the week were spent in storing and displaying their gear, maintaining their quarters, and making their beds shipshape. They also engaged in close-order drill, in physical exercises, and in small boat handling. At the end of the week, late Friday, their instructor bellowed, "You lads have a lot more to learn before retreat tomorrow. When they blow 'To the Colors' [retreat] I'm gonna meet a little Boston girl for a little recreation. And I don't wanna get drunk on my own!" The recruits smiled sheepishly, trying to cover their grins.

Sunday was a mild day, markedly warmer than Maine. The young men, scrubbed and tidy, set about on the barrack steps joshing each other and writing letters home. They were acquiring sailors' talk as they "scuttlebutted," some of them enjoying a pipe or a cigarette, while the "smoking lamp" was lit. They agreed that navy life was what they wanted, "Boats and all!"

When Monday dawned, the recruits roused themselves, washed and showered, dressed, and turned out for formation. Boats came struggling around the barracks. "I've had a rough weekend, laddies, so I'll need your cooperation. My sweet little lady jumped ship on me, and I'm afraid I had a drink or two. So bear with me, and we'll have a happy ship." With that, he announced that several of the "boys" would be going over to Charlestown Navy Yard, across Boston Harbor, where the Charles River enters the inner harbor. USS *Constitution* immortalized by the lines of "Old Ironsides" lay tied up to the dock. George would be one of the boys selected, and, as they assembled, Boats reminded them to pack their entire seabag as they might finish their training there.

Charlestown, though a much smaller facility than the base in South Boston, was a feverish installation that Monday. Every dock had vessels tied up on either side, the dry dock was open with a ship being readied for admittance, and out in the harbor more warships riding at anchor were awaiting their turns. George and his new friends were directed to one of the barracks where they doffed their seabags and were marched off to the mess hall and their first substantial food since the previous evening. Viewing the *Constitution*, even at a distance as they marched to lunch, they were awed by the venerable symbol of America's Navy. The excitement to be part of that navy served to overshadow their hunger for a brief instant.

USS *Constitution* would be the training site for the balance of their basic instruction. (The term *boot camp* had not fully crept into the language then.) The poem, "Old Ironsides" still described the battered and diminished wooden vessel they were about to board. Oliver Wendell Holmes's line, "the meteor of the ocean air...shall sweep the clouds no more" resounded with such profound effect on the Navy that she was spared being scrapped but had been essentially neglected. Enough remained of her superstructure to impress the young seamen. The cannons and most of her rigging had been removed, but her solid decks (frequently to be swabbed by the recruits), remained. Here, the trainees would learn the naval nomenclature and salty vernacular of the Navy and shipboard life. Gazing at the broad gunwales and gunports where solid oak ribs pierced the decks and defined the resolute bulkheads, George could imagine cannonballs bouncing off Old Ironsides.

In the 1930s, schoolchildren and others had been encouraged to help rescue the hallowed derelict *Constitution*. Her hull planked with hard oak from Georgia, her pine masts lifted from the forests of Maine and New Hampshire, and her keel of lignum vitae, and her live oak knees and futtocks, she slid down the ways in Boston six years after her namesake, the Constitution of the United States, was ratified in 1791. She was built as one of six frigates to provide a defensive shield against predatory raids by European nations. She served nobly against British warships in the War of 1812, often against enemy vessels that seriously out-gunned her. After the hostilities—her costs and worth validated—she was allowed to shift from station to station, from one assignment to another, maturing like a heavy, complex wine, but without purpose. At one time, she served as a "brig," a prison ship, her superstructure completely removed, her glory tarnished. Old Ironsides might have perished as a target of friendly fire by the guns of her own fleet, or simply from abandonment—save for those stirring images from the poet.

Old Ironsides
Ay, tear her tattered ensign down!
Long has it waved on high,
And many an eye has danced to see
That banner in the sky;
Beneath it rung the battle shout,
And burst the cannon's roar—
The meteor of the ocean air
Shall sweep the clouds no more.

Old Ironsides touched me, personally and emotionally, in two differing ways. I was one of those school children who contributed to her resurrection, to keeping her afloat. It was a long struggle. Her design plans had to be located in the dustbins of some naval architect's archives; surveys must be conducted of similar vessels of her period (including the USS *Constellation*, then wasting away on the Chesapeake near Baltimore), and the proper materials and talented shipbuilders procured to carry out the tasks. The need to employ skilled workers would be the most difficult to satisfy, as large-scale wooden warships had long disappeared from our navy and commercial fleets had largely moved to steel and steam before World War I.

The funding was achieved (*Constitution* remains an actively commissioned vessel in the US Navy and therefore partly funded by the federal government), the work accomplished, and she has since ridden proudly tethered to the dock in Charlestown Navy Yard. She has a celebrated Turnaround Cruise annually, where her port and starboard sides are alternately shifted to differing exposures. At approximately twenty-year intervals, she receives an overhaul and restoration.

In 1990, when I initially had thoughts of an early retirement, a friend who knew my love of ships, woodworking, and sculpture had submitted my name as a member of the restoration crew for that current twenty-year refitting. I accepted the opportunity with great inner pride (but hopefully without conceit) and on a day in October, I climbed up that gangplank and landed on the main deck. Unwittingly, I was following in my father George's footsteps.

CHAPTER 3

As currents of the Industrial Revolution stirred much of Europe and began to manifest in class turmoil and ethnic violence at the turn of the nineteenth century, Judah Ginsberg could see the writing on the wall, a questionable future for his family. Though the Ginsbergs had lived peaceably in Minsk, in eastern czarist Russia, for a generation or more, a broad new wave of social unrest fomented by political philosophers such as Karl Marx was about to disturb what quiet remained. There's little doubt that these events—and a collective memory of the vicious pogroms under which Jews and minorities were murdered, displaced, or marginalized and their people (if they survived) were ghettoed in urban enclaves—must have been much on his mind when he'd emigrated to the United States several years earlier.

Now, Judah was returning to bring his wife and children to the new land, some four thousand miles distant.

In late June of 1911, after several days travel from the East, Rachel Ginsberg and her three children reached the Central Railroad station in Hamburg, Germany. The preparations for leaving their home in Minsk had been emotionally depleting. The trip itself had been tiring, and the complexity of shepherding children, changing trains, and crossing several national boundaries had drained her spirits. However, the anticipation of meeting her husband, Judah, after a two-year absence cheered her disposition and brightened her mood. The children were overly excited not only to greet their father, but also to accompany him back to a new home in America.

Judah Ginsberg, now thirty-four, had disembarked from the SS *Cincinnati* some days earlier, and was already at the home of an acquaintance when his family arrived. Overjoyed, Ruth, the oldest of his children at age six, could not contain her thrill to see Papa and threw herself into his arms. Her two younger siblings, though, could barely remember their father but were most happy to be off the train. Judah had found a small Jewish bakery prior to their arrival and had purchased some confections sure to delight the youngsters and a *challah* for the Sabbath. That evening, before extending the goodies to his offspring, Judah offered a quiet blessing, *Borei minei mezonot,* a praise for nourishment, as well as thanksgiving for his family.

A few days later, having rested and reacquainted, the family stood on the ancient quay at St. Paul's Landungsbruecken that marked the edge of town and the river Elbe. The steamer, SS *Cincinnati*, a mainstay in the immigration trade, lay along the quay, lifting and settling rhythmically as the tide ebbed. The ship, a 582-foot liner built in Danzig in 1908, had carried Judah across to New York on its maiden trip in May 1909. Through a bullhorn, the chief steward announced that boarding for Southampton and New York would begin in half an hour, and that last-minute arrivals needed to be registered on the ship's manifest and display their proper papers and credentials. Rachel, her spirits elevated from her recent reunion with her husband, sat quietly on their baggage, her face expressionless, trying to conquer a fear welling within. If she spoke at all, it was to scold Ruth for not keeping a more careful eye on her brother and sister. Ruth, barely at the age of reason, acknowledged her responsibility but was averse to her mother's continual reprimands. A baggage handler came by and, with a steward checking their tags, placed all but their smallest bundles aboard a cart and trundled them off. The family, a party of five, was called and they walked—the children ran—to the gangplank to board the steamer. The ship must have seemed a massive hulk to the children, its black hull several stories high and dotted with rivets, its steel plates newly painted, and its baggage portal down below at dock level swallowing up hundreds of trunks and suitcases.

The chief steward, with the purser at his elbow, took his position at the entrance of the gangplank and announced in three or four languages that casting off was imminent and that all should now be aboard and guests must depart. The hawsers tying them to the quay were lifted and, with a tug nudging the ship away from the dock, the captain signaled "All ahead, slow," and the vessel was steered toward the middle of the river to pick up the channel markers. The tide had turned as they loaded, and it was now pushing them gently down the estuary toward the sea. Most of the passengers remained on deck during the departure, shouting their good-byes and gazing at the city they might never see again. When the ship reached midstream, the captain relinquished control of the ship to the first officer, who would direct the helmsman on their eight- to ten-hour trip down the estuary.

As the last vestiges of Hamburg receded, the family retreated to its third-class cabin, midship and below deck. It was a larger than usual sized cabin, designed for two or three people, but would do for their family. It was several steps up and removed from steerage, the accommodations Judah had taken on his initial trip to the United States. The family stored the few belongings they carried, each claiming a drawer or shelf and a hanger or two. The children were bouncing with pent-up energy to explore and meet others onboard. Their mother relented, partially, when she told them they could go but to "wait for your father."

On deck, Ruth held her brother Benjamin's hand while Papa secured Pauline's. They kibbitzed with a number of families and individuals, learning that several, like they, were headed for Brooklyn, NY, USA. The children's faces displayed some moderate alarm as the wooden deck beneath their feet started to quiver, and the propellers turned earnestly, pushing more water astern as the vessel surged confidently ahead. As they steamed on, the estuary widened, and the ship began to roll gently. Below in the cabin, Rachel was experiencing the first flushes of queasiness.

Nearly half of what Judah had carried aboard was food, enough to last at least a week. The foursome went below deck while the ship was still in the river channel, and Papa broke out a loaf of bread and some fresh fruit. They ate sparingly, washing it down with tea stored in a canning jar they'd brought with them. When Judah showed his wife what they were consuming, she motioned back she'd not join them. *That's all right*, he thought. *She looks a little peaked.* Her stomach didn't right itself for several days.

The Cincinnati arrived at the mouth of the Elbe estuary just before the sun set over the port bow. They passed the city of Cuxhaven on the port side and reached the Bremen coast. By now they'd be in the North Sea, setting compass for Southampton on England's southeast coast. The captain cautioned the deck officer to have all running lanterns lit and later, when crossing the English Channel, to post a lookout in the bow. The ship took on a more determined roll with the bow pitching occasionally as it tore through waves on the open waters of the North Sea.

The children were clamoring to go back on the deck, and their father obliged them. The night sky was aglitter with constellations racing like thoroughbreds across the heavens. The youngsters were astonished to see such a vast celestial display unhindered by buildings or trees. After the younger ones had nodded off, the family went below deck to sleep and to comfort Mama.

After Southampton, where the Cincinnati boarded several dozen more passengers (all in first- and second-class accommodations), a course was set for New York. The route was straight with little deviation. As they neared the North American continent, the captain cautioned his officers to keep a watchful eye for storms emerging from the south—early season hurricanes.

On the evening of July 6, they reached Sandy Hook, a spit of land off New Jersey, a few miles southwest of Lower New York Bay, and awaited daylight and a pilot ship to assist them to their destination in one of the busiest ports in the world. The harbor pilot came aboard at seven o'clock the next morning and, after a brief consultation with the captain and first officer, the ship got underway through upper New York Bay, traveling slowly but steadily for the piers at Ellis Island, the immigrant processing center and the first touch of American soil for millions seeking refuge and a new life.

Every passenger, including Rachel, came on deck as the vessel neared the Statue of Liberty. It was an emotional moment, thrillingly awesome for the Ginsberg family. In some sense it marked the culmination of a centuries-long Diaspora of the Hebrew nation.

The Ginsberg family descended the gangplank and lined up for processing. They were screened for evidence of health, and their hair, eye color and distinguishing marks were noted. Each was measured for height in foot and inches. Papa attested that none of them was an anarchist or a polygamist, and that he had in his possession $86.50. He noted that he alone could read and write in the language of the new country. Lastly, when they were asked for their final destination; Judah proudly stated the family would join him at 370 Osborn Street, Brooklyn, New York.

The borough of Brooklyn, in the city of New York, was crammed with immigrant families in July of 1911. While it had been essentially farm country before the 1830s, it was also attractive to a more genteel class of successful merchants and others who wished to enjoy the proximity of the city without the high-pitched clamor. Much of this placid scene would change with an influx of Irish families escaping the Potato Famine at home, but preferring likewise, a more subdued place to live, rather than a teeming metropolitan city. By 1887, when the Brooklyn Bridge was completed, Brooklyn had become a concerted destination for newcomers, and successive waves of Irish, Italian, and Jewish immigrants would state to inquiries at Ellis Island that Brooklyn would be their final destination. Not so Judah Ginsberg. He had his sights eventually on someplace across New York Harbor, on the New Jersey side, but Brooklyn would do for now. It would allow his family to become acclimated to a new but strange culture, customs, and language.

The children would pick up the language quickly, Judah thought, as children always do. For many of the more mature folks, it could be more difficult, as Yiddish was spoken everywhere, and it was familiar to them. It was less formidable for the men than women, as their livelihoods required them to mix frequently with English-speakers. Judah had been trained as a joiner—a specialist in wood cabinetry—in the old country, and his work would have required that he quickly learned the language of his fellow tradesmen. His proficiency in several European languages would suggest he picked up the vernacular readily.

Young Ruth enjoyed her "new" home. There were dozens of girls her age, some even from Russia. She loved learning to skip rope, by herself, and doubles with another girl, and two ropes. The boys played a strange game called stickball. Ruth would stay outside, playing and loving the feeling of freedom it gave her until—and it almost always happened—her mother cried for her to come in and watch the young ones while Mama went shopping.

The family's flat on the third floor consisted of three small rooms running the depth of the building. The front room, in which most of their daily activities occurred, overlooked Osborn Street. There was always something to observe on the street and sidewalks below, and the window seats were prized viewing spots. Ruth was sometimes posted in the window seat to watch for particular vendors, who would park their hand-pushed carts next to the sidewalk, ringing a bell to summon the housewives. After a few weeks, she was allowed to go to Fleisher's or some other market to buy provisions for the family. Returning she could be seen with a sack of groceries hanging from one hand and rolling a large hoop with the other.

Their quarters on Osborn wouldn't equate to their apartment in Minsk, but everyone was happy to be there and coping as necessary. The flat had a sink with running water, a makeshift refrigerator, and a one-burner gas stove. They shared a bath with the family across the hallway. Efficient use of the bath for a dozen people required good timing, cooperation, and an implied neighborliness.

Before bringing his family to Brooklyn, Judah had enjoyed an abundance of work in his trade within the borough, where there existed numerous fine homes. His specialty, constructing elaborate staircases largely in the homes of the wealthy, was rapidly disappearing, though, as many buildings were being converted into tenements, and people of means were moving up to Park and other avenues of Manhattan, joining others of their class in well established "silk stocking districts." He accepted that he might have to seek a different vocation—and a new home across the bay.

A year later in the summer of 1912, and with the help and encouragement of some new Jewish friends, he found what he was looking for in Bayonne, NJ. He discovered that a fair number of his faith were living there and, simultaneously, that they lacked resources—including a kosher meat market—to complement their cultural and dietary tastes. He found what he wanted, and arranged to rent, "with an option to buy," a small store on Avenue C. It was an entrepreneurial gamble in uncharted waters, but he conceded to himself that with hard work, a modicum of business savvy, and, in a bow to the spiritual and pragmatic, with the blessings of God's hand, he would succeed.

As Judah fleshed out his ideas in his mind, he acknowledged that success would be more assured if his family lived close to his work. He reasoned also that his meat market must appeal to non-Jews, who were the vast majority of Bayonne's citizens. That evening, Judah outlined his goals to his wife, after the children had fallen asleep. He didn't minimize the hazards of a new venture. He explained his business plan and added, most importantly, that everything required their moving to yet another strange city. Rachel viewed everything with caution. Judah listened carefully as she dissected his ideas, though she admitted that much of her concern was fear-based, and hadn't they experienced enough upheaval in their lives? It could have ended there, except Judah laid out the balance of his plan: a new home on the Boulevard with front and rear porches and a backyard; a wonderful school across the way; and of course, a rabbi and synagogue nearby, of which they'd be part. Rachel could see the optimism in his broad face and, warming, assured him she'd do whatever he thought best for the family. A fraction of the benediction, *Birkat hashinam* ("Bless the year for prosperity!") escaped from Judah as they concluded their conversation.

The family gathered at the ferry terminal near Brooklyn Heights, awaiting the boat to Jersey City. Once aboard, they stood on the starboard side, to better glimpse the Statue of Liberty as they cruised by. The children were giddy with excitement to be leaving a crowded tenement for a house of their own, in what Papa called, "the country." From Jersey City, the Ginsbergs rode the trolley almost to their front door at 478 Boulevard. "The" Boulevard, along with Avenues A and C, was an important thoroughfare in Bayonne and one of the three streets of its "downtown." Before the family entered the house, Judah uttered a small prayer, mostly to himself, and pulled out a homemade placket that wished all *Shalom Aleichem*. Rachel was touched as she hugged her husband and each child.

In 1912, most Americans still lived and worked in the same community, if not the same neighborhood. Possessing a means of transportation other than what the community might offer seldom presented a problem. And so it was with the Ginsberg family. Their new home on the Boulevard could not have been more convenient. Judah might not live over his store, but it was only a short stroll from home. His customers would frequently request a roast or a chicken from Mrs. Ginsberg at her home, knowing that Judah would prepare and have their order ready at the butcher shop when they ambled by.

Similar to many towns in nearby metropolitan areas, there was a demonstrable feeling of hard work leading to success. Bayonne, however, was unlike any place they'd lived before for an extended time. There was little, if any, segregation by ethnicity or religion. Next door might be an Armenian family, and several Irish families might be domiciled at the end of the block. An Italian family with six children might reside across the street. Assimilation was the goalpost for harmony among differing cultures; acceptance and accommodation could advance that objective. The public school by its very description was a key player in the ethnic matchup.

Little Ruth, after slightly more than a year in her new country, had become conversant in English, enough so that her father sought her out to explain idiomatic phrases he couldn't comprehend. The Monday following the family's arrival in Bayonne, October 12, 1912, Ruth was enrolled in Number 12 School on West 10th Street.

That morning, dressed in a freshly ironed, loose-fitting blouse with scarf and a dark skirt, she had accompanied her father to the school. Her youthful joy and enthusiasm appeared boundless as she met her teacher and was, in turn, introduced to the class. Judah lingered a moment next to the teacher before passing on some departing encouragement to Ruth to "Make your family proud." She would do so at Number 12 School, and later throughout high school.

Religion and religious life were nearly a given in America in the early 1900s, particularly in the smaller towns. While concepts of social responsibilities of religion had crept into their philosophies, the major Christian and Jewish sects were still closely tied to biblical teachings. The large majority of citizens, old and new, professed a faith, and nearly as many regularly attended a place of worship. For Jews, a bifurcation into Conservative and Orthodox branches, as well as the emergence of Reform and Reconstruction elements, complicated the practice of one's Judaical faith. For the Ginsbergs, their proclivities, especially in social matters, would have been Conservative but, pragmatically, they would have joined with the more Orthodox to worship and follow Jewish law.

One concern Judah and Rachel would have faced was how to educate their male offspring in preparation for proper manhood, that is, to facilitate their sons' literacy in Hebrew. The obligation for male children differed considerably from that expected of females. Ruth's parents would seek out a *hadarim*, an afterschool solution for the boys. (By Ruth's accounts years later, there was a pattern of her being denied opportunities that had been accorded to her younger brothers.)

In spite of gender differences, a sense of unity and happiness prevailed at home. This was particularly so when Ruth was permitted to have her new friend, Delores, over for a few hours. Delores (Dolly) shared much with Ruth: they were classmates, they had almost identical family roots, and their choices of games, dolls, and books were very similar. They were inseparable and, in the way of young girls, they adored each other! (They were destined to enjoy a lifelong friendship.)

Ruth's relationship with her father was most satisfactory. He delighted in having her come into the family store and would proudly show his customers her report cards and her childish art renderings. By the time she was in seventh grade and twelve years old, he would confide in her his personal and business concerns, much in the way a husband confers with his wife. Judah loved to tease and amuse his oldest daughter, and she would counter his playfulness with wit and laughter. Sadly, the warmth she enjoyed with her father was missing in her connection with her mother. Rachel could be affectionate with Ruth, though it lacked consistency and was often conditional. As young Ruth reached adolescence, the gap would widen.

CHAPTER 4

Miles to the north near Boston, the navy vessel USS *Samuel Bowles* had steamed around Deer Island and was headed for a mooring off Castle Island. She was scheduled to take on ammunition and a few other stores and, before sailing, to board several crewmembers, including six who had recently concluded their basic training. Her captain had received orders to join a squadron of other destroyers in a high speed run to the New York area, where they would berth at Brooklyn Navy Yard before returning north.

Meanwhile, a lighter ferrying the six new seamen and several sealed documents for the captain approached the destroyer on her lee side and tied up fore and aft under the quarterdeck to disembark her passengers. The men's seabags were thrown aboard, the sealed envelope passed to an officer, and the seamen scrambled up a Jacob's ladder to join the crew of the *Samuel Bowles*. Once on deck, seabags over their shoulders, the new crew members saluted the quarterdeck and stood before the deck officer.

This was to be a "shakedown" cruise for the *Bowles* after lengthy refitting at the Bath Iron Works in Maine. The ship and her crew would maneuver along with the other vessels in depth charge runs using live munitions ("ash cans," the sailors called them). The supplies aboard and stored, the captain went down to the quarterdeck to view the new crewmembers. As he approached, the deck officer brought the new members of the ship's company to attention. "Men," the ship's commander spoke in a clear voice, "welcome aboard the USS *Bowles*. This ship has a long history of pride and accomplishment. You've had a good training so far." He paused as he looked over the new complement. "And as you become more acquainted with your assignments and duties, you will contribute to that success story.

You'll get your sea legs shortly, but you'll be expected to 'pull your oar' every moment you're on duty. Have a good cruise!"

The deck officer, Lt J.G. Becker, added after the captain had left, "Your assignments for this cruise are posted behind me, as well as the rating to whom you'll report. I expect you to learn your tasks so they become second nature to you—so you can perform them in the dark, in a tumbling sea. And one other thing; unless you're assigned to a gun or weapons crew, stay the hell out of the way, as we'll be using live ammunition and we don't need people bumbling about!" With those stern comments, he brought the sailors to attention and dismissed them.

George Landry, along with several others, was assigned to the deck crew. Their duties varied from handling mooring lines to manning small boats to conducting "man overboard" rescues to maintaining clear and usable decks and all the duties in between. Their section leader, Petty Officer 1st Class Peterson, took the men below deck to their quarters where he assigned them their bunk spaces (a hammock "that will swing nicely to the roll!") and places to store their seabags. Each man would live entirely from his seabag—there were no lockers—and from a small ditty bag that hung from the bulkhead and stored a few toiletries and personal belongings. "Sailors in my charge will be clean shaven every morning. Water is scarce aboard a ship and you'll bathe only when directed—which won't be too often! You can scrub up and clean those dirty armpits when you're shaving! The scuttle-butt (drinking water) is in the passageway. Any questions?"

One of the men asked timidly, "When will we get to New York?"

"Forget about it, sailor, we haven't left Boston!"

The pre-World War I years were prosperous and productive for the family at 478 Boulevard. Judah, possessed with natural entrepreneurial skills, had a thriving market and had built firm relationships with the various ethnic communities in Bayonne. His store sometimes resembled a social club, with housewives and neighbors greeting and hailing one another.

At home the Ginsbergs demonstrated their continued fecundity with the addition of two more children, Irving and Silvia. For Judah and Rachel, having children, especially male offspring, was a divine blessing; it was an

assurance of continued prosperity. The fortuitous events carried an attendant obligation to which the parents fully subscribed, to raise their children
in a manner respecting both the spirit and the letter of the Torah, the first
five books of the Hebrew Bible. This posture could at times present difficulties or contravene conventional social patterns in a community that
was largely non-Hebrew, and in a nation where Jews were a tiny minority.
Though the Ginsbergs sent their children to secular school—Benjamin
and Pauline were also now enrolled in Number 12 School—they would
"keep the Torah" in most respects at home.

It was a morning in late March, when spring finally felt like spring,
when you could feel the warmth of the morning sun tingling your arms
and face. Dolly came by Ruth's home just before seven thirty to collect
her friend. They helped Ruth's mother ready two younger siblings, Ben
and Pauline, and the foursome set out for school. "Yes," Ruth's mother had
agreed, "you may go over to Dolly's for an hour or so after school (and
after bringing your brother and sister home), but I'll need you to bathe
your little brother and the baby before supper." The two seventh-grade
girls went off skipping and clutching each other's hands, Ruth's siblings
pushing on at a run in front of them.

By the time Ruth and Dolly were in seventh grade, they'd gained paren-
tal permission to go off to the theater, the library, and any number of places
nearby. What they longed to do, however, as they earned their parents'
further confidence, was to go to the city—New York City. It was, then, a
different era in metropolitan life; the trolleys and ferries to Manhattan,
and even the subways, were considered relatively safe for adolescents and
young adults, provided they used good judgment and observed a modicum
of caution. The girls admired two close friends whose parents allowed them
to go into New York, unsupervised and unchaperoned, albeit with a list of
things to avoid. Her parents, after all, Ruth remembered, had frequently
cited her precocity. At age twelve, her parents would be considering their
oldest child's *bat mitzvah* (a daughter of the Commandments), signifying
her coming of age and the formal acceptance of responsibilities and obligations as an adult. She was ready for all of that. And for New York City.

The commemoration of *bar mitzvah* for boys had become a well-established custom as early as the latter part of the sixteenth century, though

it had not, by 1917, taken on the level of celebration as we know it today. The observance for females as Ruth reached that age, however, remained perfunctory and subdued. She was informed, almost without ceremony, that she was about to cross that threshold. Her father obligingly read a brief passage in Hebrew; he then indicated an even-briefer response in English for young Ruth to read. And that was her *bat mitzvah*.

It shouldn't be assumed that her parents failed to value her elevation to womanhood. They were complying with long-established Jewish tradition. For Ruth, her new status was accompanied with more demanding duties around the Ginsberg household, but also with new opportunities at her father's store. More importantly, it created new freedoms, when away from home and when with her friend, Dolly.

At 0600 hours, the mooring lines were lifted and USS *Bowles* backed into the channel, preparing to exit Boston Harbor. The ship had received telegraphic orders, overnight, to steam easterly to a point forty-two nautical miles east of Nantucket Island and there be joined by a second destroyer already underway from Portland. The two ships were to then proceed southeasterly to a point of rendezvous some 120 miles farther south. The coordinates for meeting were verified, and the *Bowles* moved along to the channel stream. George's deck detail was assembled, and they went as a group to the mess deck below for a breakfast of fresh eggs, toast, and fried potatoes. Petty Officer Peterson cautioned his new team to eat lightly until they became accustomed to "tin can" (destroyer) life. He added, "Enjoy the good navy chow this morning while you have a level deck under you! The cooks have a way of disappearing in heavy weather, so you'll be lucky to get hot coffee."

When George's crew came up on deck, the ship was nearly abreast of Provincetown Light, at the tip of Cape Cod. The captain, on the bridge, handed over the operations to his executive officer, with orders to maintain only a moderate speed, as they awaited a position report from the other destroyer, USS *Richardson*. Using a bullhorn, the executive officer notified all within listening distance that, while this was a practice maneuver, the ship would be observing wartime conditions throughout the cruise, as live enemy submarines were not uncommon along the Atlantic seaboard.

The bridge received a coded message that their companion destroyer was already on station awaiting their arrival. Subsequently, the executive officer ordered an increase in speed from his engineering department, and the USS *Bowles* surged ahead, frothy waters leaping aside as the vessel knifed through the gray Atlantic. By late morning the two ships were joined and they plotted their course to the south.

After the call for midday mess, the executive officer ordered drills for simulated depth charge runs to commence at 1330 hours. George's crew consumed their lunch hurriedly and climbed up on the main deck. They cleaned and swept down all decks and ladders, readying all deck positions for firing exercises, and returned to their quarters. "Battle Stations" were declared by voice throughout the ship and the "tin can" proceeded to a "suspected target" (submarine) where it would release its depth charges. These would be dry runs today. Tomorrow there would be simulated runs again, but with live munitions.

Just after four bells (1800 hours), Richardson's lookouts spotted the first of the ships with which they would rendezvous. By six bells (2000 hours), they were finally assembled as a squadron. The commanding officer aboard the flagship signaled the course for the evening hours and ordered the individual ships' captains to read their sealed orders describing the exercises commencing tomorrow morning. He signaled further the necessity to maintain combat conditions with darkened ships. Lookouts were to be doubled over the hours of darkness. With the sun setting astern, the squadron steamed on an easterly course for the night.

At 0600 hours the exercise began with six destroyers in two columns, two thousand yards apart on their beams, and following at a slightly greater distance. Only the two vessels in the rear would be releasing their depth charges on each leg of the triangular course. The ships would alternate their positions within the squadron at the conclusion of each course leg. The exercise continued well into the darkness and for several days. At the termination of their maneuvers, the flag officer signaled, "Well done!" And later, "You have sunk a dozen U-Boats!" Referring to his orders, the *Bowles's* captain directed his executive officer to "steer a course for the Brooklyn Navy Yard." Her sister ship from Portland, the *Richardson*, would follow.

Petty Officer Peterson reshuffled some of the deck watches for his men, assigned details for the next morning, and invoked, "OK, mates, you can take a full-body bath in the shower; you start after your next watch, two at a time and no grumbling!"

Having finished his early morning watch, Seaman Landry came up on deck after breakfasting, looking for a secluded spot out of the breeze to reread his letters from home in Maine. One letter informed him that he now had a little sister, as his parents had agreed to take in Alice, a distant cousin orphaned by the death of her mother. George was pleased to know he had such generous parents. He was not homesick, but he missed his parents' company and the goings-on at the farm. He needed to write and tell them of the naval exercises he had just taken part in, and that they were headed for New York and liberty ashore.

George scribbled a brief letter home and read it quickly to himself, just before his section leader, Peterson, showed up in front of him. He scrambled to his feet to hear Peterson recite, "Our section is gonna be in the deck parade when we reach the Navy Yard, first row, too! Everyone in dress whites, your scarves tied properly and with clean headgear! Go down below, Landry, and relay those orders to your shipmates."

Above, on the bridge, the captain had telegraphed the harbor commander that the USS *Bowles* was approaching, that she'd expended all live munitions, and that she awaited instructions. On the main deck and below there was a flurry of activity as the sailors readied the ship for docking. George and his crewmates, freshly shaved and showered, were breaking out their dress uniforms. Their white blouses, having been carefully folded and packed in their seabags, appeared crisp and attractive, and with their black scarves tied expertly in "sailors knots," the young men looked like old hands.

As the *Bowles* nosed into New York Harbor, the captain received signals to meet with a navy tugboat for its final run to the Brooklyn Navy Yard. The men of the deck parade were piped up to the main deck while the ship was still a few miles off its berthing space. Pennants were hung from the bow to the mast just aft of the bridge, and similarly on the stern quarter. The day was pleasantly summer-like and a light breeze stirred in a nearly cloudless blue sky. An air of festivity and excitement hovered above decks, as the deck parade assembled.

Ruth and Dolly, along with two other close girlfriends, had convinced their parents that this was the ideal time for an afternoon visit to New York. It was midweek, they would travel to Brooklyn, meet with other friends in that borough and possibly—though their plan was incomplete—visit the Botanical Garden. Ruth's parents, having previously acknowledged her maturity, acquiesced pretty much without comment.

Dressed in white cotton frocks, scarves encircling their waists, and sporting broad-brimmed hats, the girls were the epitome of fair womanhood and summer as they boarded the trolley for the first leg of their trip to the city. They were giddy with the anticipation of being on their own and the freedom of being open to serendipity.

Landing at the ferry terminal in Brooklyn, the young ladies from Bayonne joined with two additional friends who lived nearby. Together, the six winsome teenagers went for lunch at an outdoor café a few blocks away. Their arrival in Brooklyn, along with hundreds of other citizens of all ages, coincided with the Navy's planned reception of several warships of the Atlantic Fleet at the navy base, virtually next door to the café. It was a fortuitous moment. Dolly, who enjoyed assuming the lead, insisted, "Why not scrub our plans and 'join the Navy?'"

The young women proceeded through the main gate, under the approving eyes of the marine sentries, and were directed to a grassy area with benches. The benches were partly shaded by two ash trees, which would be most beneficial, as the sun was climbing and the afternoon temperatures were on the rise. A destroyer was being berthed just as Dolly, Ruth and their friends seated themselves on the benches and the surrounding manicured lawn. After adjusting their skirts, they looked up into the gazes of twenty-five handsome sailors who stood at parade rest but were unable to resist eyeing six engaging females as the ship inched its way dockside. Dolly uncharacteristically stuttered as she exclaimed, "That's going to be my guy! The one in the front, next to the guy with the blue eyes!"

"OK," Ruth said. "I want to meet the young man with the blue eyes and the blond hair!"

Orders were being barked to the shore party as the vessel was secured with heavy lines, fore and aft, and a spring line attached midship for balance and stability. The women stood up, coquettishly ringing the bench as the sailors descended the plank and spread out in groups for liberty at various destinations. The men were happy to be ashore, happy to be in a stirring big city. In the background, a band was playing a spirited march, and the sailors picked up a lively step, some of them approaching the young ladies under the shade trees.

Ruth and Dolly, standing with arms around each other, suddenly realized they were now in uncharted waters. The sailors around them were close enough to touch, their warm, fresh faces reflecting equivalent male apprehensions. A sailor spoke directly to Ruth and started a conversation. She noted, as they conversed, that Dolly had commenced speaking to a young Scandinavian-looking sailor. Without explanation, as was typical of their association, Dolly and Ruth "exchanged" their new friends, seamlessly continuing the dialogue. "Oh my gosh, he's the blue-eyed blond," Ruth exclaimed to herself! Before she could finish her thoughts, Ruth Ginsberg and George Landry were looking into one another's eyes.

Ruth and George were seated together as Dolly and one of George's mates made arrangements to stroll back to the café for refreshments before the girls left Brooklyn.

At the café, the foursome took a small outdoor table and ordered ice cream sodas. A girl selling flowers ambled by and, with some gentle prodding, the boys bought a small inexpensive posy for each of the ladies. The event set them to laughing as the young ladies preened, placing the flowers by their breasts. It seemed to turn what might have been stilted conversation into an easy, comfortable banter, talking of where they had come from and of their families. The men were eager to speak about the Navy and their recent cruise, the girls beaming proudly at these clean-cut "warriors." Considering the ages of the young women, it must have occurred to all that their meeting would be transitory, that it might barely last the *Bowles's* visit to port. Nevertheless, the four, giggled and whiled away the afternoon hours, grateful for each other's carefree company. They parted, shaking hands and ardently promising to write each other.

On the journey home to Bayonne, the girls chattered, but the rhapsody of emancipation, so evident earlier in the day, had dimmed. Dolly spoke of their weekend plans, of attending the vaudeville show at the Lyceum Theatre. Ruth listened, nodding her approval, her thoughts remaining in Brooklyn.

Dolly, who shared Ruth's birth year, was slightly taller than her friend and appeared more mature. From a religious point of view, her family was more liberal, which led Dolly to be more exploring and adventurous in their relationship, more apt to be the lead. This pattern apparently was agreeable to both parties. (Ruth, as the oldest among the Ginsberg siblings, no doubt had ample opportunities to lead at home!) As the ferry chugged homeward, the two talked quietly about their new acquaintances. "Should I mention the boys to my parents?" Ruth inquired.

"Certainly not, " Dolly responded. "They'd read too much into it. And it would beg another question, 'Are they Jewish boys?'"

"You're such a good—and smart—friend," Ruth conceded. In her mind, though, the afternoon was well beyond meeting a charming and handsome young man. It was something mysterious and, to a thirteen-year-old, incomprehensible but profound.

The *Bowles* had replenished her stores, and her shore parties had returned aboard ship by midmorning on Monday. The navy band, at their master's command, commenced a series of strident marches, exhilarating the rhythm dockside. The bos'n piped the sailors on deck and the vessel prepared for imminent departure.

The captain conferred with his executive and deck officers and ascended to the bridge, awaiting the 1130 hours (seven bells) departure. At the signal, the destroyers' engines came alive, commands were given to lift all docking lines and, with the band blaring "Anchors Aweigh," the ship was expertly nudged away from the pier. Forward, the deck parade stood at attention, the ensign and pennants snapping in the fresh breeze, the sailors' collars furling animatedly above their shoulders. With a stern line attached, a tug pulled the USS *Bowles* into the main channel and maneuvered her bow, so that she was positioned to steam forward into New York Harbor. The deck parade was dismissed, and the ship's company resumed its normal activities.

With the Sandy Hook lighthouse flashing on its starboard beams, the USS *Bowles* cleared New York Harbor and headed into the open sea. Her sister ship, the *Richardson*, had accompanied the *Bowles* into Brooklyn Navy Base and was now on the return path as well, though an hour behind. The two ships would resume their depth charge exercises on the return trip to Boston, observing all the procedures and cautions they'd practiced with the larger squadron.

On the second day out from New York, Seaman Landry was finishing his watch when Peterson informed him that the deck officer would like to speak with him. This was often a routine request and George thought little of it. The officer was standing alone on the quarterdeck when George approached. "Seaman Landry, reporting sir. I've been told you wished to see me."

"Ah, yes, Landry, come into the compartment here. I need to discuss a little matter with you." They stepped into a small utility compartment just off the quarterdeck. "I've received a notification from the Bureau of Personnel and I've a few questions to ask you."

George shuffled uneasily and replied, "Yes, sir." This is *not* routine, he thought.

"Who are your parents, Landry?" to which George replied they were Alexandre and Hanna Landry. "And they're from Corinth, Maine?"

"Yes, sir." George confirmed, his nervousness showing in his posture and his speech.

"How old are you, Seaman?"

"I'm sixteen, sir," realizing he could no longer deceive the Navy.

"I'm sorry, Landry, but navy policy forbids your serving at that age. Your parents are anxious to have you home, and we've no recourse." The deck officer went on, "You have a perfect record, so you needn't worry about any punishment. You'll be processed for separation after we reach Boston. You'll be given funds to get home and any pay due you, and you'll be allowed to keep your uniform. Any questions?"

"No, sir. I'm sorry if I...." he answered quietly.

"You needn't be, sailor, you've served well. Perhaps when you're of age, you'll want to rejoin." He went on to say that the captain recommended he be placed on light duty, as he didn't wish to risk injury to an underage young man.

"Thank you, sir," George said, though his heart was exceedingly heavy. Over the next several days, his mood would change to "bittersweet, " as he realized that the discharge from the Navy opened up corresponding opportunities. He was an optimist, and his first thoughts were that he might come back to New York sooner than he had imagined.

CHAPTER 5

Throughout the summer and the early fall of 1918, the effects of a world at war were being felt across the nation, no less in Bayonne. The American people were asked to save and conserve resources, to observe "Wheatless Mondays" and "Meatless Tuesdays" to obviate the sufferings of Europeans, whose countries had been decimated by four years of seesaw war that destroyed and poisoned the lands. Judah Ginsberg was happy to comply even though it would produce fewer sales for his butcher market. About town, patriotic themes were celebrated. Men were encouraged to "get in the fight," and women and children rolled bandages and collected funds for the Red Cross. In the schools the students picked up the stridency of the drumbeat; the boys marched and practiced with wooden rifles, and the girls drilled on the exercise fields displaying coordinated gymnastics. Fortunately, hostilities would end in November, but their consequences would not. (Indeed, several of its outcomes such as the redrawing of boundaries in the Middle East, Africa, and Eastern Europe remain with us.)

Europeans—even where front lines had never appeared—were emotionally, physically, and financially depleted, their larders empty of food. Starvation loomed across several continents, a crisis that might consume both victor and vanquished alike. Surveying the devastation, world leaders gathered to convince each other that global-wide solutions must be approached to avoid such conflagration in the future.

A former mining engineer, Herbert Hoover, with worldwide contacts and exemplary organizational skills, was tapped to resolve the desperate problem of hunger. He quickly and systematically arranged the gathering, shipping, and distribution of food stores on a global scale never before witnessed. Its rapid implementation averted universal suffering and starvation for millions.

On the latter problem of war and peace, the American president Woodrow Wilson had worked on and written about conceivable solutions, which were embedded in his "Fourteen Points." The fourteenth and final item, an "association of nations," was uppermost in his plan. His scheme would have established a League of Nations, an embryonic attempt to control armaments and provide a conduit for peaceful resolutions of international disputes. As history will attest, Wilson failed to obtain the consent of the US Senate, and the League never achieved its potential of "affording mutual guarantees" to protect the political and territorial integrity of nations. Conceivably, the institution he sought could have checked the aggressiveness of a reviving Germany.

Now in high school, Ruth absorbed herself in her studies. It was not an easy task, as this was a period of increased social contacts and distractions, namely boys and extracurricular activities. As to the former, her parents cautioned her repeatedly about that most beguiling attraction, the opposite sex. The warnings most likely served to stimulate her conversations with Dolly and her other girlfriends. Both Ruth and Dolly began to share in another budding interest, their careers after high school. They had settled on nursing and, with the help of several teachers, began exploring the road to that goal.

The desire to be registered nurses may have stemmed from a wartime emphasis on nursing as a patriotic avenue for women to serve their country. An added inducement may have been the effects of the 1918-1919 influenza season, the so-called Spanish Flu. This highly infectious virus caused tens of thousands of deaths, particularly among those in military camps in this country. And it was equally devastating throughout the world. An episode in Ruth's family about that time might have also heightened her interests. Her younger brother Benjamin had been injured by a downed electrical wire and taken to nearby Bayonne Hospital. (A barber armed with rubber gloves, who had observed the accident, miraculously rescued him.) The hospital had established a nursing school only a few years beforehand. Whatever the appeal, it was deeply felt by the young women.

The silence of the guns in Europe had momentarily diverted interest for most Americans from that part of the world. Ruth and Dolly, for some reason, had developed a fascination with Latin America and were focusing in that direction. Central and South America, despite their geographic proximity to us, seldom drew the attention of the American public. Our perception for centuries—when not on our expansionist dreams of westward movement—largely dwelt on Europe. Our rootstocks for the most part originated in the Old World. When the Europeans were not at war with each other, they were our principal trading partners. We admired their great universities, our wealthier citizens traveled frequently to the Continent, and our institutions emulated their art and culture. In the aftermath of the Spanish–American War, however, with growing discontent on the Mexican borders and the construction of the Panama Canal, our vision was tilting slowly to the south.

The two high schoolers were no doubt aware of the work of Dr. Walter Reed and others in Cuba to eradicate yellow fever, as well as similar efforts in Panama to make the Canal Zone livable. They may have been familiar with—and inspired by—the dedication of Albert Schweitzer to bring modern medicine to indigenous people in West Africa (and, later in the twentieth century, to South America). High school was the entry point for their journeys to a nursing career. Biology and chemistry, of course, would provide an educational foundation, but the success in any Latin American endeavor required proficiency in the language: *Entiende usted?* The girls launched into Spanish, coding their own conversations. They were like twins, possessing a private language.

By her sophomore year, Ruth realized she must discuss her future plans with her parents. Dolly, whose family dynamic differed, had told Ruth nearly a year earlier that her parents were definitely sending her to nursing school. Ruth broached the subject obliquely with her mother. Rachel merely asked that she speak first to her father. Her avoidance of the subject left Ruth puzzled. *Didn't she care?* On a quiet winter day after school, Ruth approached Papa. His immediate reaction—no reaction— suggested he'd been expecting this query. He put his arm around her. "You know," he said, "You are my little princess. You also know you have a brother coming of age. Benjamin will celebrate his bar mitzvah shortly, and Mother and I are obligated to educate him, to send him to university. He will be the first in either of our families to go on to higher education.

The war years have not been so good for our family. We will have to strain and sacrifice to help just one child. I love you, without question. But I can't tell you we might or that we will try to help you, when I know truthfully we cannot." He was still hugging his daughter as she dried her tears and prepared to leave.

Some weeks later Rachel asked Ruth, who had avoided the subject of nursing school with her mother, if she had spoken to her father. She nodded without comment. Rachel then produced an envelope and said, "It's another letter from somebody named George." Ruth's eyes lit up as she took the letter and retreated to her room.

George and Ruth had written several letters to each other since that summer day over a year earlier. Their correspondence was typical of pen pals everywhere; there was little alluding to future plans, mostly "fond regards." Nonetheless, she enjoyed receiving them, reminding her of how pleasant he'd made her feel. In this letter George spoke of his little sister, Alice, and the happiness she had brought to the farm, adding that the family hoped one day to "meet the young lady" from the city. He went on to mention that he'd decided not to reenter the Navy but would seek work in some city, such as Boston or New York, perhaps as early as next year. Reading his lines, Ruth could feel the gloom over her own future begin to lift and her spirits brighten.

Putting down the letter, Ruth wondered if life was now, mysteriously, formulating a course for the future, a design that might well include George. The thought was comforting, like a warm quilt on a cool evening, to think that she and George were much more than ships passing in the night. Consequently, the two engaged in more frequent letter writing, each one more personal and explicit about their lives and hopes. George often mentioned a book he was reading; Ruth would insert a phrase or two in Spanish, usually playfully romantic. (George most likely understood the innuendo of her comments, as thanks to his dad he was reasonably fluent in French, which had similar language roots.) By the summer of her junior year, Ruth was confiding in Dolly that George was "kind of a friend." She hardly needed to mention it, as the correspondence from George was addressed via Dolly, to avoid those long glances at home.

August had been rainy in Maine the summer of 1921, as George decided on a Saturday to take General and the small cart for a jaunt to Bangor. They passed a few motor vehicles on their passage in, and General seemed to have become accustomed to the strange apparitions. Coming into Merchants Square, they tied up just above the farmers' market, bustling with teamsters and farmers jostling for positions along the sidewalks. Here, too, a few motor trucks competed with the horse-drawn wagons. The odor of wet hay and manure was obvious but not unpleasant to a farm boy. It assured the casual observer that animal power still reigned on the Maine farm and in the marketplace.

After purchasing from a list of butter, eggs, and produce—items their farm didn't yield—George watered General, and together they trotted off to a newsstand in Post Office Square to bring home a few newspapers including out-of-town issues like *The Boston Globe* and *The New York Sun*. Leaving Bangor by midafternoon for the return trip to Corinth, George dwelt on the stimulation he felt whenever he found himself in any urban area. As much as he drew pleasure from family and farm (and its animals), he missed the vibrancy he experienced in a city. The horse's reins lay loosely in his hands, as General strode in measured steps homeward. George, fumbling among the newspapers, glanced at the *Sun's* headlines for a moment, and his fingers came to rest on the "Help Wanted" pages. The national economy, post-World War I, was hitting its stride, and the help wanted ads reflected the enthusiasm Americans were placing in a continuing prosperity.

Once home, and after helping little Alice with the supper dishes, George retired to his room to more carefully peruse the newspapers. He was particularly drawn to the offers of employment in the railroad industry. With a booming economy, rails were chugging ahead full steam, unable to keep up with demands. The New York Central; the New York, New Haven and Hartford Line; and the Pennsylvania Railroad were mutually anxious to find new qualified workers. George wrote to all of them.

For high school students everywhere, the senior year is special. It is a brief period of things ending and things beginning. It is a moment of newly gained freedoms with promises of more to come. Ruth and Dolly had an active social life, and when the local boys came calling—usually at Dolly's home—they'd make fudge or discuss Booth Tarkington's last novel, *Seventeen*. It was an invigorating year for both genders, though few of the students had "steady" friends. The norm was to sit in the parlor or on the back porch, with a parent or older relative in the next room. If more than a casual relationship evolved, then the two were "seeing" each other. Neither Ruth nor Dolly was "seeing" anybody at the time. The girls were caught up in a swirl of activity, nevertheless, leaving little time for worrying about next year.

In late October, Ruth received a brief note from George, explaining he had taken a job with the New York Central Railroad and would be starting employment within two weeks. He added that he'd contact her again after he found a suitable boarding house and had settled in. When she informed Dolly, they simultaneously exclaimed that this development would likely hasten the remaining months of their last year. "How will we ever finish knitting our high school sweaters?" Dolly questioned. The comment produced a near convulsion of laughter.

"Don't be absurd," Ruth replied. "We can finish them when we're old ladies!"

It wouldn't be long before George came calling. He had obtained a pleasant room in a boarding house with a mixture of male students and workers in Fort Lee, New Jersey, close to his work above Manhattan. He had started employment on a crew in one of the switching yards, attaching and decoupling cars and engines, physically laborious, but appealing to an able-bodied twenty-year-old from a New England farm. George made friends easily and was feeling at home in the New York area. He and Ruth were in touch frequently, though George was slightly intimidated by the metropolitan travel system and had not visited Bayonne. The girls arranged with Dolly's family to have one more guest for Thanksgiving dinner. The young man from Maine received the invitation on a note signed by both girls with an accompanying map to help him navigate his way.

George would traverse the route often, to the point where a daunting trip became relaxing and familiar. He fit in comfortably with Ruth's friends and was fussed over by Dolly and her mother. In no time he became *the boyfriend*.

With little doubt, Ruth's parents were aware that she was seeing someone. The circuitry for gossip was an open book in a moderately sized town like Bayonne, particularly where the schools, shopping, and other institutions were close by, and children and parents intermingled daily. Her father's advice that young ladies of sixteen should avoid entanglements with young men—"wait until you've finished your schooling, and you have direction in your life," scarcely opaque, implied some knowledge of her social life. Ruth adored her father and listened to his counsel. From her mother, there was no intimation that their daughter was on some forbidden path, rather a singular quietude that only deepened the gulf between them. While Rachael was usually cordial with her eldest child, she could be abrupt, her voice lacking warmth and affection. Their wills often collided.

In the midst of familial discontent, Ruth often sought comfort at the piano. Her teacher, Mrs. Blumenthal, came by frequently and would assign her various pieces of classical music which she would delve into as time (and emotion) permitted. Hilda Blumenthal, now elderly, had been classically trained in Berlin and had performed on stage in several European cities. When she visited the Ginsberg household, she would listen to young Ruth perform a previous assignment, all the while discussing the aches and afflictions of old age with Rachel. If Ruth fumbled on a difficult passage, Hilda was quick to erupt with; "No, no, no!"

Ruth especially liked scores allowing a long musical run or a frenzied crescendo of bass. "You have good energy," Mrs. Blumenthal might compliment, "but you need to keep control. I want to hear the blending, too."

In these months, Ruth was not concerned with control. She wanted to release some pent-up emotion.

Looking through the lens of ninety years, it is tempting for some to propose an Oedipal lure existed between father and daughter, with a wife's accompanying resentment. Conversations with my mother years later convinced me that it was basically a confrontation of two strong-willed women. There were other contributors to be sure. Ruth's birth placement among the children and Rachel's strains from maintaining a large household—five children, a husband and a family business—involved duties that likely left little time or energy for intimacy. As the eldest child, Ruth was often a surrogate mother, and conflicts and animosity could have built from that. Had proper counseling been available to them, as we know it in the twenty-first century, reconciliation might have been achieved, benefiting both. Regrettably, the void between them would never narrow, the wounds only deepen. Eventually, their struggle would worsen to where there was a complete break in their relationship. Before that happened, though, there would be some lighter moments.

In Bayonne, as across America, the venerable draft animals and their teamsters were disappearing from city streets. This was particularly so in commerce, though many individuals, including those who'd have never owned a horse and carriage, were examining automobiles in great detail, whenever they might come across one. One parked near Judah's market on a bright April afternoon, and the entire butcher store emptied for a closer look at the shiny metallic contraption. Judah joined the throng. He began making inquiries and, to the surprise of his family, pronounced one evening at dinner, "We've just arranged to buy a motor car, and we're going to take a trip to the mountains!"

The reality of what their father uttered seemed far-fetched to the children, and they looked to their mother for some confirmation. "Of course, your mother and I don't know how to operate an automobile, and we're too old to learn, I think. So, Ruthie (which he seldom called her), you'll be seventeen in a few weeks, and as our oldest, we want you to become our chauffeur." Ruth beamed with gratitude for the honor they were bestowing on her.

There followed a dozen sessions of instruction: "Don't forget to push down on the clutch. Give it a little more throttle; take your hands off it when turning! Push the brake down slowly, change the gears, and release the clutch!" It was certainly challenging, but Ruth felt exhilarated and accomplished, perhaps the only member of her class to be a licensed driver of a motor vehicle.

The family's first motor trip, to the Kittanning Mountains on the New Jersey-Pennsylvania border, was daunting and a touch scary for a neophyte. Ruth gained her confidence rapidly, and by warm weather they were bouncing over farmland to the Catskills and beyond.

To be seventeen added another notable facet to a young woman's future; she would have achieved the age of legal consent to engage in many activities, including marriage. (This matter differed across the country and in some regions, such as the South, the age requirement was much lower.) Ruth gave little thought to crossing the threshold at that moment; she was just pleased that she would be freer to exert her will and conjure up and follow her dreams. She would drop the charade about her boyfriend and be more open to her parents—soon, but at the proper time.

Despite a busy summer with friends and family, Ruth and George were seeing each other at every opportunity. When George's job allowed a weekday off, the two would "do" Manhattan or take a cruise on the Hudson River. They were, without question, emotionally in love, though conventions of the day would have precluded their sleeping together. They were in every sense a couple, and they were planning their future. To this end, George was putting aside most of his earnings. He'd allowed himself a new blue serge suit and occasional books but lived frugally. When in each other's company, Ruth insisted they share expenses, so that he could put aside "every nickel." (This was an unusual attitude for women at that time, but she wanted them to plan for their life ahead.) The couple explored Manhattan economically; they visited Central Park and the Battery— even taking a peek at Hell's Kitchen and the Bowery—at the cost of a subway ticket. "You can do Manhattan on a dime," she would later boast to her own family.

By the middle of summer, George had formally proposed marriage to Ruth and she felt obligated to bring him to meet her father. *It will be complicated*, she mused, but she would never have ease of conscience if she didn't try. First, she needed to deflect the pessimism the task suggested.

George Landry in navy winter uniform, c. 1918.

Ruth Ginsberg in beach attire, c. 1922.

CHAPTER 6

The issue of presenting George to her father remained essentially a mental exercise when, some weeks later, Ruth received a brief note from George telling her he had been injured on the job and would be several days in hospital. He didn't elaborate as to the extent of his injury, but she instantly intuited that it was serious and prepared to go into the city.

Ruth entered the lobby of Roosevelt Hospital on 57th Street and was directed to George's room, which he shared with three other male patients. They embraced immediately, her fingers darting through and grooming his disheveled blond hair. He beamed, delighted to have her there. He motioned to his elevated right foot, explaining that he had a partial cast, some mild pain occasionally, but was otherwise fine. They both understood that this posed a gigantic obstacle to their plans. Ruth winced visibly, as she instinctively read his chart and put his personal things in order. His physician, making early evening rounds, entered the room accompanied by an orthopedic surgeon. The doctors introduced themselves to George and Ruth and informed the young couple that they were considering surgery with a goal of maintaining some range of motion in his foot. The plan was to amputate the toes and a section of the right foot above the metatarsus.

Before he departed, the physician discussed the procedure in more detail and offered his prognosis. "I know it's not good news, Mr. Landry, but you're otherwise young and healthy. You'll have a convalescent period, but we'll have you walking soon enough." He went on to say that, after what he had observed as an army doctor in France, "This will be more of an inconvenience than a handicap."

The couple looked at each other for several moments neither commenting. George finally broke the silence, "You know I love you—in ways I can't even describe—but it would be wrong of me to become a burden to you when your life is just opening up for you. If you feel this has changed our plans, I will understand."

She sat on the edge of his bed and replied, "When I told you I loved you, I was absolutely sincere. I wouldn't think of leaving you. We're going to make our way together, no matter the problem!" At that, the couple embraced again, tears streaking both their faces.

Presenting George seemed out of the question, when her father asked if she "was still seeing the young man. You need to know," he went on without waiting for a reply, "we are an ancient people. We wouldn't exist today if we didn't—your parents didn't—follow the Torah. You are of age now, but you still carry an obligation to your family. You'll never be less in my heart, but I cannot condone or bless your relationship."

Ruth realized that any response was futile. The position of her parents was firm; there was to be no room for accommodation. "Thank you, Papa. Thank you for all you have done for me." She kissed him gently on the cheek and turned toward the door. Her mind turned to George and their future together.

George was on the road to recovery when Ruth helped him obtain a more commodious living quarters with an Irish woman whose husband was still healing from wounds he received during the war. Mary, the boarding house landlady, assured Ruth they would have no trouble caring for the young man and that she had two strong young lads who would "help get Georgie-boy on his feet. Dearie," she added addressing Ruth, "I've a bed for you whenever you might wish to stay."

Ruth next proceeded to buy him a pair of shoes, high laced, from a merchant who asked, "Why would anybody want shoes of two different sizes?" She had reasoned, of course, that George's right foot would need abundant cushioning.

George's physician had made arrangements for him to see an orthopedist close by in New Jersey. The specialist confirmed, on George's second visit, that the healing appeared to be progressing well, and the stitches were removed. He cautioned George and Ruth that "visually everything looks quite acceptable, but it is not uncommon for infections to develop deep within the tissue where we can't observe them and most likely you cannot feel their presence. You'll need to be vigilant over the months ahead." His comments would later—regrettably—be all too prescient.

George first became ambulatory using a crutch and, after he had succeeded in putting some weight on his disabled foot, he graduated to a cane. He was pushing to get back into his life, when, with Ruth, they visited a nearby Chinese–American restaurant one evening. It was one of those early so-called "chop suey houses." Though crude of menu, it was deceptively romantic at night. A light supper was capped with, predictably, tea and fortune cookies. Ruth giggled opening her cookie, the humor of which, she declared, "only a Chinese native" might comprehend. George fumbled with his, intimating that the ring with a few small stones had fallen out of it." It was perhaps not a novel idea, but the gesture expressed sincerity and tender affection that was unambiguous. Their waiter poured a second round of tea, and the couple, misty-eyed and holding hands, planned well into the future.

Events moved swiftly over the next month. Dolly's family returned from its vacation in the Adirondacks, and she and Ruth joined in planning a momentous happening—an elopement. They approached their new assignment with vigor and enthusiasm, amusing themselves as "the twin conspirators." They would devise all the arrangements and satisfy all requirements before the ceremony. George would handle the itinerary after their "declarations to honor, love and obey," until the couple left New York and reached their destination of Bangor, Maine, on the Penobscot River.

On a late fall afternoon in 1922, Ruth chose a fashionable silk mauve dress, one with a pleated skirt and a top that fell softly over her waist. Over her short, curly, dark brown hair, she wore a pink bonnet, slipped on a long, dangling pearl necklace, then pinned to her outfit a simple gardenia corsage. Thus dressed for her wedding day, Ruth and George, marriage license in hand, met with Dolly and a male companion at the law offices of Geoffrey P. Griffith, Esq. and Honorable Justice of the Peace. Attorney Griffith, in a moment of charity, declined his fee. Observing the youth of the newlyweds, he gave them some fatherly advice: "Life will be tough enough for you; you must save your money." It was hugs and kisses as the elevator descended, to the slight embarrassment of the lift operator.

The wedding party then headed for Delmonico's, though Dolly's friend politely begged off as he had previous plans.

At the restaurant, George disclosed a hand-written, well-advised menu for this celebratory dinner, which began with a creamy lobster bisque lightly laced with Madeira. When they reached the dessert course, their waiter placed before them an Italian sparkling wine, beautifully presented in cut crystal tulip stemware courtesy of the maître d'. It was "superior to any French champagne," the waiter boasted. The three finished their dinner with a warm glow induced by the joys of the day, as well as the sparkling wine from Italy.

As they retreated to the street, a bittersweet moment swept the young ladies. The two had considered each other best of friends since meeting in grammar school. Now, the realization of a long parting produced a touchingly sad moment, and for several teary minutes they clung to each other, recounting the antics they'd hatched and the joys they'd shared. George stood aside, but his eyes were misting as well. Letting go of Ruth's hands, Dolly turned to leave. She pleaded with the newlyweds, "Don't let me sadden or interfere with your wedding night. I love you both."

"We love you, too," Ruth and George chorused. They watched her depart, to be separated from them by time and distance in the unknowable future.

Late that evening, at the Keller Hotel, Ruth blissfully placed her gardenia in a small tumbler, declaring that she was decorating their first domicile. The hotel on Barrow Street overlooked the Hudson River and was adjacent to the piers, where two days later they would board a coastal steamer for their trip to Maine. In the meantime, the couple would spend a few enchanting days in the city, attending a matinee at the theater, lunch at a German beer garden, and a shopping trip to Macy's department store.

Their hiatus over, they prepared to leave the hotel, but not before Ruth pressed the gardenia into a small notebook she carried. She reminded George to leave a generous tip for "the working girl," and they descended to the lobby, checked their luggage, and climbed on a tram for Washington Square. Upon their arrival, they took a brief measured stroll through the square, noting an abundance of late blooming roses and then sat at a small café's outdoor table for a leisurely lunch. The sun was warm and nourishing as they watched doves and squirrels competing for crumbs on the stone terrace. It aroused a poignant memory of a day, four years previously, when they had met for the first time in Brooklyn.

The couple returned to the Keller, just after three o'clock, and took a hack to the pier. Their baggage was placed aboard the *Falmouth*, the Eastern Steamship Line's vessel that plied the coastal waters to New England. George and Ruth walked up the gangplank and met the first officer. "Ah," he uttered, "you must be the young couple who've just been wed." He stated they would be in the stateroom number twelve on the first deck and would dine with the second sitting, about seven thirty. "We'll be putting you ashore in Boston, where you'll pick up the packet for the trip to Bangor tomorrow."

When they went to the purser's office for their meal vouchers, they were told the captain "graciously requests" the newlyweds at his table. George, his arm about Ruth's waist, murmured, "We're a couple of lucky stiffs!" acknowledging, that with all the difficulties they had faced, this was a memorable gift of good fortune. Ruth replied, using her personal term for overwhelming gratitude, that she was "pinched with pleasure."

The captain, pink-faced and sporting a handlebar mustache, presided that evening over a table of eight. His eyes sparkled as he praised George and Ruth as honeymooners who preferred Maine to the Pocono Mountains or Niagara Falls. "You exhibited good judgment," he said and, with the table joining him, predicted that the couple "will have a long life together and many beautiful children." His comments were trailing off as Ruth glanced down at the beautiful table setting in front of her. The linens, the silver, the porcelain plates and chargers, the gorgeous cut-crystal stemware and finger bowls were all agleam from the lantern light overhead. She sought George's hand beneath the table. It was as impressive, she remembered over the years, "as the finest dining room in New York."

After dining, the couple joined several other young people strolling the main deck. The air was cool but comfortably so, as the other young folks, one couple at a time, disappeared, and George and Ruth stood watching the eastern shore of Long Island flickering into darkness and the heavens opening with their evening performance. Reaching their quarters, Ruth asked, "Can we always be this happy?"

In Boston, the next afternoon, the couple boarded the *Bangor Packet* for the trip Down East. The packet reached Portland early the following morning where, after discharging several dozen passengers and embarking a few others, she left for an all-day run along the Maine coast. Cruising six to ten miles off the mainland, the passengers were treated to the magic of the coast—islands upon islands, green with pointed firs. The packet ran close under the eastern rocky cliffs of Monhegan Island and, at the Matinicus Lighthouse, steered north for Rockland and the opening of Penobscot Bay. After tying up at the pier in Rockland and boarding a number of summer visitors, the captain stated that the ship would overnight there and depart at six the next morning. He explained that he needed daylight to navigate the river, but that the passengers could enjoy another splendid day of sight-seeing, with the vessel cruising at four to five knots upstream.

The next morning, the ship pushed off the Rockland pier, with the emerald Camden Hills slipping by their stern quarter, and headed for the sailing channel north of Pulpit Harbor. The course through the islands of Penobscot Bay was mesmerizing in the morning light, with here and there a white sail signifying a private yacht, silhouetted against the green hills. At Castine, an officer announced that luncheon would commence shortly, and George and Ruth went to their stateroom to freshen up for their final meal aboard ship. They sat again with their loquacious captain, as he described the river beyond Bucksport. "The helmsman must stay alert, 'cause we're not in a good bargaining position in a narrow river. But don't worry, the old *Bangor Packet* has a mind of her own and knows the way."

From the earliest times, the Penobscot River had figured in the lives of Maine people. Like its sister rivers, the Kennebec and the Androscoggin, it provided an entry point for those nascent overseas adventurers for first exploring and then utilizing the vast, heavily forested interior of the region, which until 1820 had been tethered to Massachusetts. Before the turn of the eighteenth century, Maine had been valued chiefly for its deepwater ports, its fisheries, and its hearty band of sailors. For the struggling British colonies of a century earlier, Maine also provided a handy buffer against threats and provocations from French Canada to the north.

As cities on the Atlantic seaboard grew, the demand for timber, quarried stone, and bricks, along with vessels to carry them, led to development inland. Though many of those industries were in decline by 1922, there was still much evidence of their former glory in the small towns that nestled on the water's edge, and here and there fortifications built to protect the river from British marauders in the Revolutionary and 1812 eras.

George could feel they were nearing their destination when Ruth sighted numerous church steeples penetrating the cloudless sky just ahead and to their left. She could not have compared it to anyplace she had ever lived as she viewed the warehouses, the rail station, and the merchants' quarters that crowded the river shore. But instinctively, she knew she was home. On a rise just above the wharf, a lone, older gentleman, idle reins in his hands, waited for his son and "new daughter."

CHAPTER 7

George's mother, Hannah, could not have been more overjoyed than to welcome a daughter-in-law that September. Hannah actually insisted that Ruth call her "Lizzie," as many of her friends had done before her own marriage. Lizzie showed her "daughter" about the house, including the new ell where the newlyweds would be bedded. Alice, who had been taken in by George's parents while he was in the Navy, was just folding up a quilt she and Lizzie had made over the summer, a gift for the new family member. Ruth emerged from the house tour with the arms of her mother-in-law and "cousin" close about her waist, with George beaming approval of his wife's reception. Alex, not to be out done by the others, brought out his violin, promising to play *une petite chanson française* after dinner.

The couple slept late (by country time) into the morning, aroused only when Alice knocked quietly and cracked open their door so that aromas of coffee and breakfast on the stove were abundantly evident. Looking out her window to the meadow in the back of the farmyard, Ruth could see what her husband had so often described, a happy General nibbling grasses, his tail whisking contentedly. She kissed her spouse for having brought her to this special place.

Alex and Lizzie insisted that the couple stay with them several weeks or "as much time as you would like." They gladly accepted the offer but affirmed their wish was to find a place in Bangor. Accordingly, they drove off a week later, with General proudly pulling the carriage, to what would be their first married residence.

After several fruitless quests, they found what they were looking for, a sturdy-looking Greek gothic structure on May Street, a block from the wharves and Union Station, and steps away from the Bangor House and other notable homes. The house had been built by a prominent local family, and its large rooms and bays, its white-columned front portico, symbolized an important resident. The house had recently been divided. This new home, where they would be tenants at will, comprised the entire first floor. Ruth, who maintained that a house was not a home unless it contained flowers, proceeded to a flower and nursery shop a few minutes' walk by foot and brought two red geranium plants still in full bloom. She was cautioned by the shop attendant that there'd be frost within days and be alert to that threat. Ruth accepted her advice and bore the plants home, placing them on either side of the front entrance.

In Maine, if you've not planned already, and "brought in" for a long and cold winter, the first frost is a clear harbinger of what's to come. George set about gathering storm windows, repairing exterior walls (where necessary), and blocking off unneeded spaces to mitigate the effects of a wintry season, where the temperature might plunge below zero frequently. He ordered two cords of firewood from Connor's Woodyard, across the river and, when it came, chucked it into the basement, a rear shed, and a small amount into the front hallway.

Ruth occupied herself with scrubbing floors and woodwork, lining kitchen shelves with colorful papers, and searching basement and attic for useful furnishings. In the attic, she found a trove of a previous family's toys, bric-a-brac, and wall hangings, much of which she brought down to "give character to our little home." On one of her forages, she discovered a hidden closet. When George pried open its stubborn door, she beheld an antiquated, foot-operated Singer sewing machine. Through their joint efforts, the implement became operational, and she immersed herself in curtain making. Fortunately, several rooms contained paneled "Indian shutters" that provided privacy, while affording a modicum of protection from the cold outside. Out of the basement, they carried chairs and a breakfast table, as well as assorted cooking utensils and serving dishes. (When George informed his landlord of their findings, he was told, "If it is useful to you, it's yours.") "This is great fun," Ruth told her husband, "making use of what others have discarded." They were proud of their preparedness for the ides of October and the advancement of another season.

In the meantime, while the magic of fall foliage continued, they hired a horse and carriage from a livery stable on Kenduskeag Avenue and went out on an informal schedule to George's parents for Sunday dinners. Ruth savored learning her way about the kitchen with Lizzie and Alice. Together, Ruth and Alice would bake yeast breads and pies from the dough batches her mother-in-law had worked up earlier in the morning. Ruth was happily finding a mother she'd never had.

On Mondays, the young couple would return to Bangor fortified with loaves of bread and perhaps a French apple pie baked with raisins, its crust shiny with buttercream frosting. On one trip home, after having been passed by an automobile—and looking into the future—Ruth suggested they consider buying a motor vehicle (not, of course, until they had the money). "But," George replied, level-eyed, "I'll need to learn to drive the damned thing first."

Simultaneously with establishing their first home, George had been seeking employment. He wanted something that would challenge his abilities and have a promising future. He had pursued an opening with the Bangor Hydro Company, in its retail appliance division, which he felt was a "good fit," only to lose out, as he later learned, to somebody less qualified but who better suited the existing "old boy" network. He told Ruth he'd not allow himself to be discouraged. Within days of that disappointment, he received a letter from the Maytag Company of Newton, Iowa, with an offer of an interview in Portland with its district manager.

Maytag, whose name has become synonymous with kitchen equipment, had a modest beginning, wherein two farm enthusiasts, Frederick Maytag and George Parsons, collaborated on several wooden tub contraptions for "clothes washing" around 1893, one of which they called "Hired Girl." By 1920 their machine had acquired a metallic sophistication and was powered by a small gasoline engine, ideal for rural families.

His interview went smoothly that day, and George was offered a sales position to begin in late April. An added bonus to the job was the inclusion of a Ford motor car! Alluding to the applicant's country beginnings, the Maytag official cited the fact that "two farm boys started this company!"

George was thrilled with the employment offer and explained to Ruth the delay in starting was because the job included considerable travel and Maine weather and road conditions at that time precluded travel in the winter months. A few days later they walked to the Bangor Motor Company and hired an automobile for George's first driving lesson.

There is little that separates late fall in Eastern Maine from the commencement of winter. In some years a heavy rain eliminates the glories of fall in one cruel, wet overnight, leaving but the bronze leaves of the oak trees, some of which will limp on through the year's end. The days are just above freezing and the nights just below that mark. It is invigorating weather. The housewives are gathering apples and root crops from under the mass of frost-killed vegetation lying prostrate in the family garden; the husbands climbing ladders to install second-floor storm windows, after having placed banking boards around the home's foundation; and the hunter wishing for a light snowfall, to lead him more stealthily to his quarry. Some folks ask, incredibly, "When's it gonna snow?" A few would acknowledge, regrettably, "But I haven't got my wood in yet!" The wiser would maintain, "It's going to warm up a little before it snows." These were all reasonable questions and assertions in the early years of the twentieth century.

The demarcation of winter, according to local lore, is simply "a little after Thanksgiving." In November of 1922, the family gathered at George and Ruth's, partly as a housewarming, for Thanksgiving. The bride, at her insistence, cooked the entire meal with all its festive trimmings, including her special dessert, a delectable cranberry pie with a lattice top crust. Whether it was a great success has never been recorded, but the cranberry pie would continue for decades on our family holiday menu.

When the snows came that winter, they stayed. By Christmas over two feet had accumulated, with drifting causing numerous blocked roads. A stillness prevailed, a Currier and Ives quietude, broken only by a few pedestrians, scarves flung about their necks, crunching over the sidewalks. An occasional horse and sleigh would glide along the street, amplifying that winter scenario. The motorcar, in these early years of the twentieth century, had for the moment lost its mobility. Ice and snow buildup, ideal for horse and sleigh, was anathema to the automobile. Consequently, the owners of these glamorous new machines placed them in their "recycled" horse barns, up on blocks with their radiators drained to await warmer weather, the horses turned out to pasture elsewhere and the sleighs and carriages stored in a loft above. A few automobiles, such as taxies and municipal vehicles, might prowl the streets, but a general calm prevailed. The preferred, and sometimes only, travel out of town was the railroad. In Maine, dependable contact with the outside world was consistently maintained by the Maine Central Railroad.

George inventoried his woodpile from day to day, hoping a predicted "January thaw" would extend their fuel resources. Ruth closed off rooms not needed and pulled blanket curtains over the windows to keep the cold at bay. It was essentially a balancing act, maintaining just enough heat to preserve indoor plants and keep the water pipes from freezing. She would later boast "that as the temperature dropped we snuggled more deeply!" And, presumably, she never lost her geraniums.

The vernal equinox signals the start of spring in many regions. Blossomtime in Maine that year, however, was illusory, and Mainers sat like disheartened Cinderellas, impatiently awaiting the return of their spring flowers. But slowly warming temperatures had broken the ice in the river, and bare streets and sidewalks were evident throughout the city. George recommenced his driving lessons and by early April Ruth admitted, admiringly, "You're going to be a better driver than I am!"

At the end of the month, the ground bursting with daffodils and jonquils, and iris shoots filling the flower beds, George and Ruth boarded the train for Portland, their spirits high, as they anticipated his new career. The Maytag office was charmed by the couple, revealing that they were seldom introduced to their employees' wives. While George huddled late that morning with his new boss, Ruth inquired and received instructions on the care and operation of Maytag's iconic square-tubbed washing machine.

The economy of the United States was booming in 1923, while much of the world remained in economic shock, devastated by a worldwide conflict that had ended and left vast regions in shambles. American agriculture, manufacturing, and a bustling oil and auto industry put discretionary income into the pockets of its citizens, enabling housewives to consider improvements to their homes and kitchens. The Maytag Company—and a budding appliance industry—were well positioned to assist the homemaker, who'd long been neglected by technological advancements. Her husband, Ruth felt, would be on the cusp of this new wave of prosperity.

His meeting finished, George cranked up the Model-T Ford coupe, customized with a small compartment for transporting appliances, and they headed for the high road, the Maytag logo prominently displayed on both side doors. Driving home, a smiling George rhapsodized over the clamor of the engine, "Ruth, we're a couple of lucky dogs!"

Ruth and George—and the woodpile—had outlasted their first winter, but just barely. They found a smaller, more compact house in Hermon, on the outskirts of Bangor, and moved there in June. It may have been disappointing to relocate from May Street and a home they'd so lovingly brought back to life, but they swiftly mustered their energies, and the little cottage, not unlike his parents' farmhouse in nearby Corinth, was restored with bright wallpaper, gleaming enamel, and freshly scrubbed and varnished floors. George built screens for the rear porch where, he promised lyrically, they "could watch the heavens and listen to the crickets chirping in the evening."

As the seasons changed, George hired a local woodsman to cut, split and deliver their firewood, explaining to Ruth he'd need to re-split much of it for their finicky little stove, but only when the wood was cold and dry. By late November, Ruth watched as her husband, after spitting on his hands and wielding the axe high overhead, let it come crashing down in one smooth movement, rendering each block into two, and assuring them of a warm kitchen. The couple had achieved a charming, livable home, made ready for winter, when Ruth announced, "George, I think I'm pregnant!"

"Dear Dolly," Ruth would write, "I've so much to tell you...."

There was a flurry of activity, now, both at home for the expectant couple, and at George's parents' in Corinth. George and Ruth decided that their dining area, off the living room, would be an ideal nursery. In the spring, when the roads were passable, they visited his parents, and Ruth, together with Lizzie and young Alice, knitted, wove, and sewed garments and coverings for the eagerly anticipated arrival. Lizzie had long retired from her service as a midwife, but her delight at being a grandmother transcended all obstacles of age. She pitched in with enthusiasm to prepare her daughter-in-law for motherhood. "Now, you must eat well, my dear," she instructed, "And you must avoid any heavy lifting. George will be wonderful around the house for you." She predicted that, "with all the signs, you'll be blossoming by the middle of July."

On July 16, 1924, Ruth labored, winced, and pushed out a beautiful baby girl into the hands of a loving midwife and mother-in-law.

The infant, to be christened, Lorraine Elizabeth Landry, would be my oldest sister and her parents, my mother and father. After the physician arrived later that day and nodded approval of all that had taken place, my dad was allowed to hold the infant for a moment. He took the baby easily in his two hands and, when she cried lustily, he placed her back on her mother's bosom. "Ruth," he said, "we're now a family!"

My mother had kept up a tenuous relationship in Bayonne with her own family, through letters to Dolly and several female cousins. The news of a baby granddaughter arrived there within days of the event. Her father, Judah, with a radiant smile, accepted the news, though he and Rachael had virtually severed all contact. He told friends he'd never become accustomed to the "loss" of his oldest child. The birth of Lorraine underscored the absence he felt for his Princess Ruth. *Could I*, he wondered, *convince her to return to their home where a loving family could care for her and her child?*

In early November, Judah put himself on the train out of Grand Central Station in New York, carrying a dilapidated suitcase that had crossed the Atlantic several times. He transferred with his baggage in Boston and again in Portland, declining a porter's help. (He claimed he'd not sufficient change!) He arrived in Bangor hauling his bag and registered at the Penobscot Exchange Hotel telling the desk clerk, "It might be a few days." He surveyed the lobby, found a desk and scribbled a brief note to his daughter that ended, "Love, Papa, and I hope you'll bring your baby with you."

My mother, as she would later relate, was both surprised and uncertain of her response. "What did he expect?" My dad, equally mystified, suggested she should at least see her father, which she did.

It was a tearful reunion. Their emotions could not disguise the hurt they each felt over their separation. "Best not to talk about it," he suggested.

His intentions became clearer: would she agree to return with him to Bayonne? It seemed an open-ended offering.

She felt conflicted. Hadn't she punished her parents already? She would have to bring her baby with her of course. "My first loyalty has to be with George," she spouted, "Let me talk to my husband, and we'll let you know."

If my dad was fearful of losing my mother, he never let on. "But we don't want a lot of regrets to deal with in our future, so I'll not stand in your way," he offered graciously. "I can't tell you how much I will miss you—and our little Lorraine."

Lorraine was a toddler, slightly advanced for her age, when George bid his wife and daughter good-bye, having formally met Judah only a moment before. Their meeting was cordial but brief, as Ruth stood observing the two most important men in her life. Holding her child, Ruth embraced George, as the conductor shouted, "All aboard for Portland, Boston, and New York." Their cheerfulness couldn't obscure the significance of their tender parting.

Having previously spent but an occasional night away from the family's Bayonne home, Ruth enjoyed seeing her siblings and catching up with cousins and friends. George and Ruth resumed a correspondence, much as they had years before, and the bond and affection they held for each other was seemingly unbreakable. After several weeks and much conversation, Ruth's family was dissuaded of all thoughts of separating her from her husband and their home in Maine.

Three days before Christmas, (Kris Kringle as my father would have it), mother and child boarded the train to Boston. She'd not return to Bayonne for another fourteen years. They stayed overnight at the Manger Hotel, near Boston's North Station, and reboarded Boston & Maine's train for Portland (and Bangor), arriving into George's joyful arms at 4:45 p.m.

By the mid-1920s, profound changes were occurring across the country: Americans were moving off the farm; women had gained the vote, more social freedoms, and more respect for their economic contributions; and the automobile and a system of roads to accommodate it, along with developing air travel, were modifying the environment, transmuting the very sights and sounds of everyday living. Within three years, Maytag had stationed George—and a growing family—in three different communities. The couple's first son, Robert Eugene, came along in 1925, and George Jr. followed in 1927; they were my oldest two brothers.

Had the booming success of the post-Great War period continued for a few more years, and had the division of wealth it created been more fairly distributed, an economy the envy of the world might have emerged. As it happened, prosperity was only marginally evident in some levels of social and economic life, but middle-class Americans could at last consider acquiring more and better material things. For those with wealth whose desire for concrete things had been satiated, there was wild speculation in the public stock markets and the banks, as well as a belief in an ever-upward economy. There were other areas of concern as well. Farm production and incomes were in slow declines, and in many arid areas of the central and midwestern states, a continued drought and brewing dust storms were darkening the skies of the established order.

In the Plains states, such as Oklahoma, rural folks were indeed dealing with dust storms that had devastated their farms and uprooted families. With several years of crop failure and dust swirling up against their homes, tens of thousands of farmers and their families (rudely referred to as *Okies)* were in an exodus to California and points in the Northwest—most to an uncertain future. These trends and forces would coalesce in the fall of 1929.

Woody Guthrie, folk songwriter, poet, and voice of that era, fittingly captured the magnitude of those storms and the resiliency of rural Americans with his lines from "Dust Can't Kill Me":

This old dust storm it's a-kickin' up hardrock,
Kickin' up loose dirt from sea to sea,
If this old dirt blinds me, I still can feel ya,
It cain't stop me.

This old dust storm it's a-diggin' my farm up,
This old dirty dust storm it's a-chokin' me.
Money man broke me and this weather might break him,
But it cain't stop me, girl, it cain't stop me.

While storms might erupt like an errant cloudburst for many families, my parents, given their frugality, were at least partially prepared for the ending of good times. My mother's mantra of "Save for a rainy day" and my father's habit of stashing away coins in a small purse he kept in his left pants pocket would suggest they were reasonably prepared for the downturn. What they were not prepared for—and had set their hopes against—was a recurrence of problems with my father's right foot, which had been partially amputated several years earlier.

It began with a mild ache one evening, but by midday had become moderately painful. By the second day, there was no denying that there was a serious problem—likely infection—in the foot. They entered the emergency room at Eastern Maine General Hospital in Bangor, Eastern Maine's only substantial medical facility, with guarded optimism, trying to bolster one another's confidence. Without the benefits of contemporary imaging techniques, it would seem by conjecture that exploratory surgery was employed and the source of infection located. And without antibiotics, the offending tissues were treated and a drain of some sort established. This would inaugurate a series of treatments over many months. Eventually, with hopes for treatment fading, and the onset of gangrene, a further amputation was unavoidable.

Throughout these months, my father would show his cheerful side, my mother would later quip, and would constantly show his deep concern for her and the children. On the evening before the procedure, the orthopedic surgeon consulted with the couple, indicating the region where the amputation would take place: at a point one-third down the shaft of the tibia, well above the diseased area, but located as to not inordinately disturb muscle tissues. The recovery time would be more extensive than the foot surgery, but the hospital had established a physical therapy program that would offer help as long as he needed it. "I'll bring a stiff upper lip," Dad promised. "I've been there before, Ruth." They would need that resolve, but they assured each other they'd survive this setback, as they had others.

The operation went well, and the surgeon's prognosis proved to be correct. Convalescence would be months, not weeks. After the site of the surgical sectioning had healed and the muscle strengthened, a prosthesis was shaped and fitted, and the long sessions of relearning how to walk began. As my mother remembered, "The hospital couldn't have been nicer!" The doctors and staff, informed of Dad's fondness for reading, brought dozens of books to his room. "An entire library," she said. As he gained mobility, he was given, "kitchen privileges," which he enjoyed as he bantered with the cooks and observed the bustling activity of meal preparation. My parents admitted that their lives had been altered, the process of establishing home, career and family derailed for a time. They would, they promised, plan for their future, nonetheless.

Throughout his bouts with injuries and medical procedures, the New York Central Railroad stood by him and assumed responsibility for the costs he'd accrued. It didn't likely reflect a largess on the part of the railroad. It probably came about because of a more worker-friendly environment, pushed in no small way by American labor unions, and a more understanding, and more progressive stance by the federal government. The company had offered a modest settlement to my father for his injuries, in addition, but my parents hesitated to accept it until they could see Dad's route to recovery more clearly.

CHAPTER 8

The years 1923 through 1928 had been exciting but turbulent years for George and Ruth. In addition to fathering three children, George had undergone major surgeries, initiated life with a prosthesis, and somehow managed to provide financially for an expanding family. For Ruth, in addition to three healthy children, she had borne two others who'd died in infancy, one of whom, Dolly, had been honored with the name of her life-long friend, Delores. Childbearing itself can be exhausting, and the loss of two children must have been an additional and devastating blow for the young couple. The grief surrounding these losses was apparently internalized, never to surface in family conversation. For Ruth, these arduous times also entailed moving several times to unfamiliar towns and the daunting task of making a sometimes shabby house into a welcoming home. To that end, the Singer sewing machine would be called into action, and attractive new curtains would appear almost magically throughout the new residence.

George's physical disability required several lengthy periods of recovery, and his employer, the Maytag Company, while empathetic, was reluctantly obliged to lay him off several times. This was still a period when workers had few protections from the caprices of economic life or the arbitrary whims of an employer; this did not apply to the Maytag Company as much as to the prevailing notions of political and industrial responsibility.

Whenever a rough patch might appear in their road—and they would materialize all too frequently—the couple's determination was to face adversity head-on. And a stronger family would emerge.

It is worth stating that my parents were not endowed with special gifts of wisdom or intellect that ultimately led to family success. Rather, it was more their cooperative spirit, coupled with his unbounded optimism and her sensible caution, that allowed them to persevere and achieve. "Ruth," George would say, "we just need to tighten our belts! And move on."

A long with the good fortunes of most of its citizens, the American visual horizon was rapidly changing. The motorcar had become commonplace, and visions of a national road system were slowly emerging. The airplane, though not yet a reliable means of transport, was achieving startling goals of speed and endurance. One May morning in 1927, a young man from Minnesota crept into his silvery, burnished aluminum craft and began a brilliant journey of thirty-nine hours and thirty-three minutes, bridging the Atlantic to Paris. His feat would land him firmly in the hearts of people throughout the world. In America, interest in Charles Lindbergh would only be rivaled by Babe Ruth's pursuit of sixty home runs for the New York Yankees.

Lindbergh's nonstop stunt was a seminal moment for aviation and, as if it were needed, an additional impetus for American industry to churn out more goods. The economy was definitely robust and sunny, the skies azure with promise. Here and there a gray cloud might flirt above the horizon or a whiff of warm air might stir a whirl of dust on the Central Plains, but these solitary events would dissipate readily, and the good times would roll on.

D uring an earlier part of this period, in May 1926, George set out from Old Town, north of Bangor, where they'd spent the winter, and headed for Ellsworth in his jaunty Ford roadster with its prominent "Maytag" logo. He was on a new assignment for his company following a period of convalescence, and he felt revived physically and mentally as he drove in the clear bright morning, the air tinged with odors of earth awakening. He'd just passed the hamlet of Clewleyville in Holden when, approaching a curve in the dirt road, he spied a farmhouse for sale. Before this moment, his thoughts were on how vigorous and restored he felt, how with the windows open and the fresh breeze striking his face, his spirits soaring, he was back on course. He slowed to a stop and craned his neck to more fully see the little green farmhouse. Thinking critically, he reminded himself that he'd "left country living a decade ago. I'm on my way to Ellsworth."

That brief stop should have been the end of that particular intrusion, but it wasn't. George should have acknowledged that while he'd separated from the farm and rural living, "country" was still in his blood. The following April, having made a critical but independent decision, he bundled the family into the car and showed Ruth the little green farmhouse on a curve in the road, exclaiming, "We need a place to put our feet down, even if we must travel about. I've bought it for *us!*"

Ruth was the conscience for the couple. Like her mother, she was usually suspicious of any transaction of money or property. She didn't immediately respond to George's disclosure. When he dared glance at her, her lips were sealed, but he did observe a deliberate swallowing, as if she were digesting the effects this new development might have on them. Had he been more observant, he could not have missed her shoe tapping the ground, as she frequently did when some objection was flowing through her mind. "Well," she replied, "the children will be of school age in just a year or two. I suppose we'll need a more permanent residence."

As pointed out, Ruth was cautious like her mother. Ruth, however, was much more considerate of George's feelings than Rachel was of her husband. Her mother could be compassionless when refuting Judah, leading often to long silences in their household.

At length George felt his actions had been affirmed and, with 'Rainey and Bobbie in tow, the couple was soon deciding where gardens and chickens might go, where to plant the tulips and the lilies. "We'll want roses by the front corners of the house," she softly commanded, "and forsythia out by the road." George smiled broadly in deference to his wife. He'd won her approval.

Privately she thought, *I want my husband to be happy, but I know in my heart we'll not be wanting to stay here more than a few years. We'll want more for our children—and ourselves.*

It would not be until late the next summer, after Ruth had delivered another son, George, Jr., and Lorraine was being prepared to enter kindergarten, that the family moved into the farmhouse in Holden. During the intervening months, they had taken an apartment on Hancock Street in Ellsworth, which Ruth quickly transformed into a bright and warm living space, curtains and all. Ellsworth was the shire town of Hancock

County and, though small, the only town of consequence in the region. The family found itself conveniently situated with stores and a hospital a short walk away.

George quickly embraced his new sales territory encompassing most of Hancock County and the shoreland Down East. He was enchanted with the denizens of the various villages, their customs, and their peculiar dialects. He enjoyed interfacing with farmers, fishermen, and lumbermen, and with their wives. He spoke their language. Ruth would anticipate his homecoming, as he brought with him gifts of fresh cod or a pail of clams just hours out of the mud flats.

As the weather warmed that spring, George began his commute each weekend to their future home in Holden. Much as he had in each of their past domiciles, he planted, cultivated, and watered their newly laid out gardens, hoping they "could eat the fruits of their labor" come summer and throughout the winter. Their agricultural pursuits, while challenging, were not only sources of nourishment, but restorative of mind and body, *almost a privilege*, he thought.

By the time the couple moved in, however, the property, though seductive from the road, had lost a measure of its charm. The farmhouse possessed a dug well but no indoor plumbing. Electric power lines were at least three miles away. The house's foundation, bulkhead, and other elements needed repairs or replacement, and the barn needed a new roof. "We can manage," Ruth assured them both, "though it'll be a continuous struggle!"

George allowed himself to be more optimistic. He went immediately to work, rebuilding the kitchen and preparing for winter. "If I can keep my family warm and well fed," he insisted, "they can live here contentedly" despite numerous deprivations. On a bright note, he'd returned the Maytag vehicle—which he was hesitant to use—to their agent in Bangor and brought home a beautifully polished and enameled Essex sedan, an older model from the Hudson Motor Company to be sure, but a handsome maroon motor car with black trim to sit in their driveway. *We may be well out of town*, he thought, *but we'll not want to be divorced from it*!

During these years, George's parents had continued to live on their farm in Corinth, where George had grown up. In their sixties, they, like their horse, General, were living a life of ease and quiet contemplation.

That is until Lizzie, suffering from gallbladder illness, succumbed before the doctors at Eastern Maine General Hospital could save her. It must have been a stressful—and exceedingly painful end-of-life ride in the wagon for Alex's beloved wife. It proved a sudden and tragic loss for George and Ruth as well, and for a while diminished their newfound joy in Holden. They invited a grieving Alex to join them, though he didn't presently accept their invitation. *Non*, he told them, he needed time to put his farm in order.

Despite the setbacks thrown at them, George and Ruth maintained their usual cheerful outlooks and dispositions. Here in Holden, they found what they scarcely knew they needed, a healing ground where they might quietly reconnoiter and build an investment for their future. For the first time in their peripatetic lives, they had a home of their own, though, as events might prove, not for an extended time.

Nevertheless, the two proceeded to make their farmhouse livable. They removed wallpaper, scraped away layers of aging paint, and scrubbed through decades of neglect to find a patina on the wide plank floors that pleased them. The house was several steps down from Ruth's more cosmopolitan upbringing in New York, but she discovered unexpected joy in paring their lives down to the essential but pleasing minimums. She smiled to herself as she placed on open shelves the antique serving plates from Scotland—a gift from her now deceased mother-in-law. "You'll be the third generation to care for these," Lizzie had told her. "But don't hesitate to use them."

"She must be smiling down at us," Ruth whispered to herself, as she arranged field flowers in a pint-sized jelly jar on the kitchen table.

Watching from the little parlor room, where he'd been cleaning the stove, George cautioned, "The enamel paint on the table might be a bit tacky! I just finished it last night."

When asked if he'd finished repairing their bed, he said he'd retied everything, but they'd need a new mattress. "It hasn't hindered us from making babies," he added, a bit insensitively. But Ruth laughed anyhow.

"Little green farmhouse" on the curve in the road.

CHAPTER 9

The lyrics of a then popular song suggested America had found "the sunny side of the street." The metaphor was an appropriate figure of speech, but common knowledge would have implied that where sunshine and good times prevailed on one side, shadows and hard times might predominate across the way.

In the months leading up to October 1929, there were few messages of a looming calamity that the average Maine citizen might comprehend. The manipulations of the New York Stock Exchange occupied little space in the *Bangor Daily News* that fall. Even the most astute of readers would merely glimpse into the financial world before checking the sports page for news of baseball's run for the pennant and the upcoming World Series.

The onset of the Great Depression from late October to early November 1929, historically well-documented with tragedies among brokers and bankers and big investors, caused hardly a ripple in Maine, at least initially. As stocks tumbled some 48 percent on the major exchanges, Mainers were more immediately concerned with the prospects of a killing frost and with putting their homes in order for winter.

There were numerous remarks from prominent business and government leaders suggesting the hysteria in the marketplace was displaced, that the fundamentals of credit and banking were correct, and they called for calm and patience. And there would be some limited resurgence, but basically the trend was downward. Within three years, the Dow Jones index would spiral down like an out-of-control aircraft.

As the financial structure collapsed, production and jobs began to disappear. Back in Newton, Iowa, the little Maytag Company was struggling to keep its doors open, as it labored against diminishing sales. The company summoned George to Portland in the spring and informed him he'd be let go—again!

The road home to Holden that night was long and foreboding, even though he'd sensed it coming. For the young man and his family, it was a crushing blow. Ruth could see the worry in George's face the moment he stepped out of the roadster. He attempted to be matter-of-fact about his misfortune, but the fear was there in his eyes, even more so when he averted her gaze. "We can't let this defeat us!" she said, seizing the moment. "Before we get down on ourselves, let's take stock of what we have, let's count our blessings!" And they would be blessed again, as Ruth, expectant with my brother Floyd, placed George's hand on her tummy.

Ruth had already put the children to bed, and she and George, now with arms around each other, looked in on their sleeping daughter and two sons. "We are fortunate," George uttered, almost apologetically.

"Let's have something warming and special," Ruth proposed, pulling out a flask of whiskey she'd been saving. She mixed a jigger of the spirits over a small chunk of ice, added a splash of ginger ale and stated, "If we put our heads together, we can survive anything. We're on a beautiful little farm—despite its shortcomings—so we'll not starve."

George knew instinctively that when his wife was determined, they could accomplish the impossible. That evening, their pillow talk having dwelt on family plans for the coming year, the couple slept well, happy that life would flow on, a good chapter to follow one of adversity. After her morning walk with Lorraine and Bobby to the one-room schoolhouse, Ruth returned to find George gaily humming and preparing their breakfast of eggs with fried potatoes and onions to be consumed on the porch. The air felt comfortably warm as the sun rose above the grove of pines and white birches to the east, beyond the stream gushing with spring runoff. As they sat on the edge of the porch, their feet firmly on the soil, George described his garden plan, sketched out hastily on the reverse side of his "Notice of Temporary Termination of Employment" from the Maytag Company. It may not have occurred to them at that moment, but they were, at least metaphorically, on the rebound.

When the earth had warmed sufficiently, George engaged his neighbor, Mr. Rowell, to till a half-acre for the family garden. With 'Rainey and Bobby passing him seed, he planted the crops he had outlined earlier. After several days, as sweat gathered on his forehead and trickled down his nose, he surveyed the almost finished task. "If the weather cooperates, we'll have peas by the Fourth of July, and lettuce as well." A few weeks later, with danger of frost receding, he set out his tomatoes and other vulnerable plants. It had been a daunting job, even if he were a strong, physically able young man, but he felt a great satisfaction as he glanced at the verdant quilt spreading about him. "The children," he said, "have been a great help."

Before returning to the house, George knelt as if in prayer and ran his hands through the brownish earth. He'd never gardened with more beautiful soil. George needn't have been a geologist to understand that the rushing stream sweeping under the bridge and through the field had, over the millennia, deposited a surfeit of rich loams of unusual depth, rich with organic matter. It had formed contours of gently sloping terrain on his property and created almost prairie-like fields for Mr. Rowell to the north. The soils in that region were easily turned by the plow, and, because of their drainage and moisture-holding properties, forgiving to the caprices of weather—often a farmer's dilemma. "Blessed, indeed," George whispered thankfully.

Although living on the farm may sound compelling to some—even romantic—the reality can be much harsher and more demanding. There are limitations brought about by soil and climate. (George couldn't grow cantaloupe which he dearly loved.) Likewise, the couple had to rein in their ambitions, planting only what they could reasonably care for and foregoing thoughts of large animals such as a cow or horse, though chickens would be manageable. As it happened, a flock of geese had already laid claim to the waters in the stream, prompting George to predict, "We've got Christmas dinner swimming by!"

It would be a tricky business, providing a sufficiency in the larder to last the winter—at least until the earliest of nature's gifts of fiddleheads, tender shoots of dandelions, and sweet wild strawberries arrived to supplement the meager root vegetables remaining in the root cellar! It is impossible to produce all that you consume on the family farm, even in the matter of food alone. Flour and sugar for bread and sweet things, meat and fish for adequate protein, not to mention condiments of every kind will also be needed. For all these things, a farmer wants cash. As back-to-the-earth enthusiasts of the twentieth century might admit, one needs savings or an income stream to acquire other necessities of life.

With the first cool nights of late August forecasting the cyclic rotation of the seasons, Maine farm families intuitively began a retreat from their fields to their homesteads. For George and Ruth, their first summer had been a benediction; an output of vegetables steadily consumed, and abundance canned in quart-size jars now covering the shelves in the cool, stone-lined cellar. Root crops, meanwhile, continued to mature in the rich soils along the slope. As September approached, George wondered if the children might be anxious about attending school. "They've had so much fun gardening with me all summer," he said.

Earlier in the summer, Ruth had borne Floyd, her fourth child, and her first without the loving care of her mother-in-law. The birth had seemed almost routine. George had taken over the meal preparations and "ordered" that his wife not scrub or lift anything. Visioning a full larder in their brightly refinished kitchen, she felt an indescribable gratitude. "All this, a loving husband, and now four children!"

The bountiful harvest had barely been put away, when a touring car bearing New Jersey plates pulled into the farmhouse driveway. It contained Ruth's brothers, Benjamin and Irving. She had known of an impending visit but in the confusion of restoring an old house and birthing a child, she had all but forgotten their coming. No matter, she and George were thrilled to have family with them for a time.

Benjamin—or as our family would forever remember him, Uncle Ben—had just finished at the university, and this was to be a celebratory trip to visit his older sister. He'd talked Irving into coming along, and the pair had spruced up the grand old motorcar that now sat imposingly next to the Essex. The young men had finished a daunting trip, "pioneering" a nearly absent road system. "We navigated from filling station to filling station, repairing one tire and asking for the road to Boston, then Portland, and so forth," related Irving. They slept in "tourist cabins," occasionally accepting a free breakfast, in what might be considered a precursor to the now familiar B&B system. Most meals were acquired by going downtown where "you'll see the diner, you can't miss it!"

Before reaching Brewer and searching for Eastern Avenue, which would lead to Holden and their sister's house, the brothers stopped at Sklar's Market in Bangor. They procured several bottles of red wine (from an undisclosed source—this being the era of Prohibition) and assorted delicacies such as smoked salmon, creamed cheese, and blintzes. These were extravagances Ruth had not dared dream about.

Later that first evening, with light fading and the children asleep, the adults returned to the porch. Benjamin and Irving were still clad in their tweed jackets and knickers with argyle stockings They must have seemed slightly out-of-place as they perched next to George, who had retained his faded, blue overalls, though he'd added his favorite sweatshirt. Ruth had reentered the house and, to honor her brothers, had slipped on a perky, freshly ironed frock, with a delicate flounce on its hem.

The brothers smiled broadly in admiration of their sister when she reappeared. George, having opened the gift of red wine, was inspired to toast, "To your sister, my wife, and your adorable niece and nephews." It had been seven years since Ruth had seen her family—or even heard from them—and their conversation dwelt on forgiveness and on missing one another. The foursome soon focused on more amusing themes: self-effacing tales about themselves, as well as stories of the daunting road trip through New York and New England. While they chatted, they sipped wine from Grandma Lizzie's petite sherry glasses. As they prepared to end the evening, having talked much and consumed a modest amount of wine, a loon in some distant pond let out its haunting, piercing cry. George, seeing the startled looks on the city boys' faces, assured them, "That's just country living!"

CHAPTER 10

The dust from Uncle Ben's touring car had hardly settled—they'd driven back to New Jersey—when George motored out to Corinth, returning with Alex. "*Non,*" he had told them, he was not moving in with his son and family. "*C'est juste une visite,*" he insisted. George winked at Ruth, telling her later that Alex "truly wants to be with us, as a family."

There would be numerous questions about Alex's well-being and the disposition of the farm in Corinth. After several days, the conversation turned to the prospects of living and farming there in Holden. Inspecting the house and barn, Alex began to exhibit doubt as to the feasibility of restoring and living on the property. He pointed out a staggering amount of work that still needed to be accomplished, from foundation to roof, and implied metaphorically they were "putting good money after bad!" George, usually optimistic about rescuing old structures, was crushed to hear his father's comments. Ruth, on the other hand, had found a fellow traveler and couldn't resist agreeing with her father-in-law. Alex summed up his comments with a suggestion—though their present venture was justified because of circumstances—that they seek a home in town. If they were to build their own house, he'd be pleased to help them.

This discussion between father and son had proceeded pretty much in Alex's French-Canadian patois, with occasional lapses into English. Ruth could discern, from Alex's swaying of his mustachioed face and his palms turned upward, that there was no objective argument. Grandpapa was right! With a nod to Ruth, he told George he'd have "*une épouse très satisfait, aussi. Non?*" Ruth was staying politely out of the *tete-a-tete*, but Alex's affirmation of her thinking caused her mouth to curl upward in a furtive smile.

When George reconsidered his father's comments in the succeeding days, he realized the correctness of the argument and latched on to the proposition of "building a home," and of doing so with Papa. George reasoned, further, he could give up one dream for another. In any event, these talks turned out to be pivotal moments for my parents, a probable end to a peripatetic life.

The couple was on the same page and a firm blueprint had been laid out. They would seek a building site in town—either in Bangor or Brewer. Alex would sell his Corinth farm. They would continue living in and improving their Holden farm, even as George searched for the "right place," so as to increase its resale value. The site would have ample space for trees, lawn, and a garden while situated in a pleasant neighborhood with access to schools and a market. The lot should be large enough to accommodate a moderately sized house and garage, along with a separate cottage for Alex.

George initiated the hunt that fall, before the first snowfall, north and west of Bangor. He found any number of fields and farmhouses for sale, evidencing the hard times local farmers were going through. Spotting a prospective property from the road, he would filter the offering through a now-familiar lens: "Would Ruth be excited by it?" As the answers were continually, "No!" he felt a vague sense of discouragement and became weary of the task.

On one of these down days, feeling frazzled, he drove downtown in Bangor and, finding a small diner on Central Street, decided to restart his mission. He needed to be more discriminating, more selective. He was sipping coffee, awaiting his favorite "grilled cheese and crispy bacon, please," when he focused on the Kirstein Real Estate sign across the way: "We can help you find it!"

After lunch, George climbed the stairs to the realtor's office. He caught Mrs. Kirstein's eye, and she invited him to pull up a chair. As he did so, she apologized that her husband, the owner, was "out of the office, but if you'll bear with me, perhaps I can help you."

George described his search, and she produced a limited number of offerings, none of which raised his hopes." I wish my husband were here; he'd be so much more helpful. He carries a lot of stuff in his head, so I can't access it," she explained. George nodded his understanding and told himself he'd at least found a better means of inquiry. Though his initial effort was unsuccessful, Mrs. Kirstein insisted they'd find what he was looking for!

Some weeks later, Alex agreed he'd spend the winter. By this time the little farmhouse was bulging, filled to capacity and confirming their resolve to move on. Papa would return to Corinth in the spring and bring back his treasured green toolbox, it having been on hiatus for several years. For Alex, the prospect of working with his son filled him with unbounded joy.

The winter of 1930–31 was uneventful, at least for farm families experienced in rural living. January and February saw temperatures rarely above freezing and some weeks not above zero, at night. The region around Holden received its usual abundance of snow, and most roads were closed due to extreme drifting. Even with red snow fences lining much of the road, the snow accumulation went up and over these obstacles. An occasional thaw might come along for a day or two, but the rain it produced would glaze over the countryside, making a trip to the woodshed or the outhouse hazardous. It could have been looked at as a time of isolation and a generator of "cabin fever," but in the Landry household, with children to care for and entertain, it brought out Alex and his violin, dancing a woodman's jig, stomping with his boots while fiddling away. On other nights, Ruth would introduce "His Master's Voice" (a hand-wound Victrola), and she and George would dance, to the children's delight.

Another highlight of the season was the slaughter of several pigs by Mr. Rowell, their neighbor. For their help and other considerations (vegetable swapping), George and Alex went home with a half a pig. Though Ruth was not a big fan of pork, she knew it meant the family would have ample meat throughout the cold months. Nothing was wasted; the ham bone became the basis of a pea soup, and the head of the pig would provide hog's head cheese, a delicacy. Infrequently, news or mail would drift in from the outside world, and life changed its tenor for a moment. As time wore on, a wish might be made, only to be followed by, "Wait until spring!"

Out by the road, the buds on the forsythia had begun displaying brilliant yellows when George and his dad drove to Corinth to close up his parents' farm, returning with the green tool box tied firmly above the rear bumper of the Essex. On the drive back to Holden, the two decided to proceed out

Chamberlain Street, rather than taking their customary State Street route. George drove past the Excelsior School, past Alice Farrington's house, and up a moderate hill. On the hilltop, a neat dairy farm and white clapboard houses, built generations earlier, stood firmly on the left to the east. On the right, there were two houses of a different period—one a handsome Victorian with numerous gables—and then open fields for some distance.

It was late afternoon, and Ruth and the children awaited them, but the appeal of the hilltop was such that George momentarily stopped the vehicle in order to savor the special spot. Alex must have read his mind and commented, *"Parfait ! "*

It was premature to have done so, but neither George nor Alex could resist disclosing what they'd discovered to Ruth. The news made her giddy with excitement but, predictably she cautioned, "We'd best keep our fingers crossed till there is more certainty."

In the aftermath of seeing the hilltop, George wrote to the Kirsteins, who found that the field was owned by a Mr. Holyoke who lived nearby on State Street. The realtor added, "He might be willing to sell."

The morning following the receipt of the above information, George dressed in coat and tie—his favorite blue polka-dotted tie—and set out to find Mr. Holyoke. But first, he thought, "I'll go by the place on Chamberlain and get a better feel for it. Maybe walk a bit of it." He parked the Essex on the shoulder, got out, and stood glancing at the expanse of newly green fields as he fumbled for a Chesterfield. He hadn't yet lit it when the local dairy farmer, walking a team of workhorses back to the barn, stopped to speak to the well-dressed gentleman.

"I'm Lou Dougherty," the farmer offered, as he pulled a cigarette out of the bib pocket on his overalls. He scratched a wooden match on the underside of his pants and lit both. Lou was the epitome of the Maine country-man: stocky, barrel-chested, his upper arms nearly the size of some men's thighs. Holding the reins of his animals, he tucked the cigarette into the corner of his mouth, where it would reside throughout their conversation.

"Rugged horses," George noted. "Belgians?" In spite of his city attire, he and Lou talked easily, sharing stories about farming. George told him he was interested in a portion of the field and that he'd be seeking to speak to Mr. Holyoke.

"Right there," Lou pointed. "That big white house with the barn," Mr. Holyoke, he went on, owned the entire field, some thirty acres. The Holyoke family had owned a swath of land at one time, all the way from the river, he explained, his hand sweeping across the sky. "Got any children?" Lou asked. "We're five now, seems we have one every year."

George chuckled and said that Ruth had borne number four. "I guess we're both lucky."

"I think you'll like our neighborhood, quiet people, everybody minds his own business. Oh, and by the way, I'll fill in that ditch for you," he suggested when he noted George assessing the difficulty of walking into the field. The butt still clenched firmly in his mouth, Lou bid George good-bye, and stepped off with his team.

George took a deep puff and decided he'd walk the field after Mr. Dougherty filled it.

Samuel Holyoke, now well into his eighties, lived in a gracious but unpretentious home on Brewer's State Street. It had an imposing carriage barn and, together with the house, the property indicating a man of means and success. His daughter, Mrs. Brown, whose family now shared the venerable residence with Mr. Holyoke, met George at the door and ushered him down the dimly lit hallway to a settee opposite an open door, where an older gentleman, his back to the opening, hunched over an ancient mahogany desk.

"Father," the daughter said, "George Landry is here to speak to you."

"Send the young man in," the octogenarian ordered.

George entered and stood by a heavy English side chair, the only seat available. Frail, his head balding, Holyoke continued fussing over some papers he'd been studying, his long, gnarled fingers lightly tapping the desk surface. He lowered his spectacles after a moment and scrutinized his visitor. "Nice to meet you, Mr. Landry. How can I help you?"

Before George could respond, Mr. Holyoke went into a long discourse on his family's history of brickmaking and how the field in back of his home had been spared from the clay-digging process.

The old man continued his recitation with some history and insights. A century and a half earlier, Colonel John Brewer—explorer, soldier, and seeker of fortunes—had sized up the low river banks as ideal for shipbuild-ing. Others like the Holyokes, Littlefields, and Doughertys trekked a short distance inland and discovered clay, immense fields of it and tens of feet deep. When clay is dry, it is stone-like. Over eons it may become metamor-phic rock: marble or slate. When wet it is pliable and plastic. Baked in kilns it can be made into a uniform construction material—brick.

As the older gentleman paused in the one-way conversation, he rhapso-dized, "Boston was built with Brewer brick, you know."

It was clearly evident that the Kirsteins had informed the Holyokes of George's impending visit. When signaled by his host to sit down, George placed his felt fedora neatly on the credenza and sat, eye-to-eye, across from the older gentleman. "Well," George began, "I was hoping to talk about buying some land from you." He pointed in the direction of the field.

"You don't have three thousand dollars in your pocket, do you?" Holyoke asked mischievously, implying he'd like to sell the entire acreage. He went on to disclose his hopes that the Dougherty brothers might have an interest in buying the field, as it was most suitable for farming. The ongoing Depression had nixed that consideration, and so he'd listed it quietly with Mr. Kirstein. "There's little interest in land today, nobody's building!"

To the question of three thousand dollars, George answered, "No, sir. An acre or so would do for us." He could sense accommodation in the old man's gaze and continued, "We'll likely build this summer."

The conversation had become encouraging for both parties, and Mr. Holyoke reached for a plot map boxed with several others under his desk. The two men agreed on a site, marked 159, near the Ford family, and diago-nally across the way from the Doughertys' farm. "I'll need two hundred and fifty dollars for that lot, and I'll draw up the papers." He told George, "You can drop off some earnest money—twenty bucks—to my daughter, before the end of the week."

George winced at the deal he was accepting, while acknowledging that this was a huge step forward. The purchase would prove to be well within their savings, but it would strain their funds for construction. The finances of home construction and ownership would have to be dealt with later. This was Step One.

The financial side of real estate ventures must have been daunting in the early thirties. Banks were already in trouble. Even if the prospective builder could find an institution with lending capabilities, they would be hesitant to put up funds until the house had been built—so no construction loans. To increase their financial credibility, George obtained part-time employment that spring in Bangor.

CHAPTER 11

After some considerable study during the previous winter and early spring, George and Ruth had selected the design of a wood-framed bungalow to be built on their property—wherever that might be. The style was more prevalent in the West than in New England, but its compact size and functionality was very appealing to the couple, whose finances were limited. The design featured three or four bedrooms, separate dining and living rooms, and a large kitchen, yet just under five hundred square feet on each floor.

When the ground thawed in early April, George engaged Lou Dougherty to excavate the foundation at 159 Chamberlain. Lou had anticipated the work and described how, with a horse and scraper, he'd scoop out the cellar hole to the specified depth. George admired Lou not only for his eagerness to be helpful, but for the ingenuity he employed in adapting his team and equipment to any task. When the scraping operation was concluded, George hired a crew of laborers to dig out the recesses Mr. Dougherty had difficulty reaching, as well as excavating trenches for the foundation footing and water and sewer lines. Unemployment was rampant everywhere, and the men were happy to obtain work.

Before spring rains could challenge the work, George and his father built the foundation's forms that another team of workers would fill with hand-mixed and poured concrete. When the mixture was firm, he and Alex tore the forms apart, preserving the pine boards for use as subflooring on the floor above, the type of economy they would employ throughout the construction process. "We have to bring Ruth and the children in to see this," George said, as the two stood back admiring the completion of the first stages.

Ruth could only view a raw concrete foundation, but she exclaimed it was "a dream."

Though it might have been ludicrous, George boasted, "If the weather cooperates, we'll be moving in by July." This was more than wishful thinking. It was a vital consideration, for the couple having four children already, were expecting a fifth child in July. (*Moi!*)

Subsequent stages of construction went smoothly, and the exterior walls and gables were in place, thrusting into the air by mid-May. Before another week, the house was ready to accept its rafters and roof. It was at this stage, though, that George and his father ceded some of the work to another team honoring Ruth's plea that they not work high up. Shortly thereafter, with the rafters arching gracefully outward and the roof sheathing firmly nailed, George sent men aloft to attach the black asphalt shingles. There would be plentiful work yet to do, but now they could labor under all conditions, protected from the elements.

Good carpenters love to do finish work, on the exterior of the house as well as within. A crowning moment on this site would be the placement of brackets, beautifully crafted, under the overhangs of both gable ends. Squinting upward, Alex affirmed that the house now possessed a personality. George agreed but suggested they quickly install windows and trim boards, so they "might take a breather."

The men had sweated on the worksite for nearly six weeks, seven days a week, taking little more than mealtime breaks. They and the family were ready for a holiday, as they drove off to Field's Pond for the day, the last week of May. There the two men hired a row boat, ran out their fishing lines and sat patiently, talking about everything and...nothing. They'd caught no fish, apparently not even a nibble, but as explained happily, they'd shared a *grand* bottle of Narragansett Ale. It was, added Alex, "*tres bonne,*" as he wiped his sleeve against his moustache.

The children had been fed and were frolicking on the shore, as the adults seated themselves on blankets and Ruth passed out the sliced chicken sandwiches, still cold, from the picnic basket. As the children straggled back from the beach, she bid them to take their naps. As the last child, Lorraine, yawned and rolled over asleep, Ruth and the two men finished the remainder of red wine Benjamin had given them. Like the children, they fell into a light slumber. It was a refreshing and reinvigorating moment for the family.

Back in early May, after George and his father initiated work on the new house, George visited Dr. Weymouth and arranged for him to attend Ruth, who was now in her last trimester. Franklin Weymouth, MD, was one of a small handful of general practitioners who tended to the health and welfare of Brewer's citizens and to many of those in surrounding towns. The GP or general practitioner, an almost lost specialty of medicine in the twenty-first century, was alive and well in the 1930s. The GP, generally synonymous with "family doctor" was usually the first—and sometimes only—medical professional people would approach. He could set bones, deliver babies, or tend to an ear infection, seamlessly moving from one discipline to another. There were specialists in Bangor, because of its Eastern Maine General Hospital, and its resources and professionals were without doubt relied upon for the more serious cases. In George's case, however, Dr. Weymouth was confident of a good outcome, and he suggested George call on Mrs. Bertha Wedge, a registered nurse, with whom he'd worked frequently, to assist the family in the interim.

Mrs. Wedge lived at the end of a nearby cul-de-sac, only minutes away from where the new Landry home was being constructed. She visited Ruth out at the Holden farm shortly after Dr. Weymouth's notification, examining her with skillful hands well trained in both nursing and midwifery. "Ruth," she said, "I think the delivery date you mentioned of mid-July is a little off. You'll likely go into labor within a week."

With Bertha Wedge's revelation, George and Alex hastily set about finishing floors and partitions and readying the house for occupancy. The plumbing and electrical fixtures had been installed, and a working kitchen was in place. "You'll notice a few shortcomings," George told his wife, "but it beats where and how we've been living." With the help of new neighbors in both Brewer and Holden, they were in the house before June had ended.

The summer solstice had passed two weeks earlier, and the morning of July Fourth dawned to find the Ford boys next door, now in their teens, rushing through breakfast and morning chores, so they might get their bags of fireworks, go out on the street, and with a violent roar, wake the neighborhood. They hadn't reckoned with Bertha Wedge, however. When

Bertha appeared at the Landry home just before daylight to check on her charge, she spotted the young men emerging from their back shed door and heading excitedly for the street, where they hoped to ignite their ordinance. "I don't want to spoil your fun, but we've an expectant mother in the house and appreciate your going down the hill to have your fun."

The boys looked at each other for a moment and then at Mrs. Wedge, who stood defiantly in the middle of the dirt road, her arms crossed, like a sentinel. One of the lads eventually quipped, "Yes, ma'am," and they trooped off, to create mayhem down below.

Bertha Wedge knew how to structure the household for the coming event. The older children were breakfasted and then bundled off to Mrs. Dougherty's, where she would care for them throughout the day. Floyd, barely out of infancy, would stay in the house with the nurse. George and Alex got the signal and disappeared to the rear of the property. They were building Alex's cottage in the back corner of the lot, and the hiatus from working on the main house was perfect for that purpose. When the men returned to the house for lunch, Mrs. Wedge motioned George to fetch Dr. Weymouth and told him Ruth was experiencing labor.

The sun was still well above its horizon when, with the doctor's approval, Bertha, both coaching and helping the mother maintain a partially upright position, lifted the newborn out and into the waning daylight. It had been a cephalic birth, head entering the pelvis first, and, as nearly 95 percent of births are, considered perfectly normal. Dr. Weymouth cut the umbilical cord and, as he tucked it in, congratulated Nurse Wedge on her dexterity.

Ruth sat back against the pillows exhausted but happy. The doctor examined her after Bertha had cleansed the birth area and told the mother she'd not need stitches this time around. She sighed with relief.

Dr. Weymouth consulted with Mrs. Wedge, who had said she'd be available to the family as long as they needed her. He then excused himself, saying his wife expected him home for dinner. I lay cradled in my mother's arms, as she nourished me.

"We are now a family of seven," my father announced, "and I'm hungry, too!"

So much had transpired in such a short time, "We need to take our time, take stock of what's happening in our family," my mother urged.

"Fortunately, most of it's wonderful: new home, new neighborhood new baby!"

"Had he been a girl, you wanted to name her Pauline, after your sister."

"Yes, and we did want a girl, as a companion for Lorraine."

"Well," Dad said, he'd considered the name Edmund, a distant relative, but now "I'm thinking about Paul. What do you think?"

"Oh, I like Paul, very much. How about Paul Edmund?" So, after a brief conference, that was my name. "Wouldn't you like to see your brother, Paul?" my siblings were asked. I was never made aware of their reaction. But I'd been born on the Fourth of July, and I'd claim celebrity for that.

Mom recovered quickly from the ordeal of having a child and was soon back in charge. She'd accepted the temporary help of an older woman to cook and care for the children, but soon found that the older children, namely 'Rainey and Bobby, resented the strange woman with strange ways. "She can't warm toast or crackers without burning them," 'Rainey complained. My arrival must have compounded the moving-in process, so the woman's help, though brief, must have been appreciated, as it helped our mother avoid chaos.

Dad was concerned about Alex's well-being with all the turmoil going on in our household. His parents had always lived quietly, and he now feared that Alex might be overwhelmed with a large and growing family. *Au contraire,* his father assured him ; he delighted in the children. Nevertheless, my father felt they needed to finish the little cottage as soon as possible, so "Grandpa" had some independence and quiet.

The little cottage stood proudly on the back corner of the property, its cedar wood-shingled walls soon to take on a gray patina. Its bright green doors and window sashes and its black asphalt roof matched those of the main house. For the trim, Grandpa had insisted on a burnt orange enamel, a typically Gallic but subtle choice. It stood there like a jewel that summer in a necklace of green fields.

When Dad commenced painting the main house—ivory cream with green sashes and doors—Grandpa moved inside his cottage, finishing the interior with matched pine boards. It would have neither electricity nor plumbing—Grandpa was happy with that—and he would have to come into the house frequently. The cottage would basically be his sleeping quarters, but it would have a small wood stove and a cellar hole, accessed by a trap door in the floor, to store a jug of water or a piece of his favorite apple pie, for added comfort.

When Grandpa Alex had finished his work on the cottage and Dad the house painting, the two concentrated on constructing a shed to shield the rear steps and fabricating window boxes for the front of the house. The shed was more than a utilitarian space for hats and coats and skis and whatever, though it would serve those purposes. It was a space for an overflow of people and energy. Screened in in the summer, it was a marvelous spot to watch the sun setting in the west or, for my parents after we children were sleeping, to sit close together on the steps, enjoying a gin and tonic and talking—continuously—about plans for the future.

Mother couldn't wait, it seemed, for the window boxes; she'd already arranged her geraniums in pots under the front windows. Dad had delivered a large box of cow manure from the Doughertys, and he'd mixed it with topsoil to create plant material for Mom. Mother would place me under 'Rainey's careful eye and spend what time she could—before I wailed to be fed—planting window boxes, rock gardens, and shrubbery. My parents particularly loved hydrangeas and what would soon become beautiful "snowball" trees, anchored both our front and back yards to the west. There was to be only a semblance of a lawn, my parents decided, until more urgent matters (like Mom's flowers!) had been seen to. It was therefore given over to wildflowers and field grasses in the initial years. It truly must have been charming and, in some respects, ahead of its times.

Chamberlain Street and its hilltop was a most advantageous place for my parents to have chosen. It was close knit, with only five homes before my parents built and moved in. With my family's arrival, there would be some thirteen children under age ten. All six homes essentially bordered one another, so that outdoor children's activities often became group affairs, with children's voices ringing in the air constantly. The Doughertys—actually, there were two families, Hugh and Louis—were very kind and generous folks. Their farm and fields, within certain limits, were open to all in the neighborhood, and for us children it was a virtual playground. Besides the Fords, there were the Spragues, whose sons were older like the Fords' boys, and whom we barely knew. The last of the neighborhood houses was that of Lila Curtis, a retired school teacher, of whom my parents would become both solicitous and fond over the years. Because my mother's family was remote and my father was fundamentally an only child, the hilltop became our extended family, our grandfather notwithstanding.

A year or so after my parents moved to their new home on Chamberlain Street, a young family with several children—the husband's specialty was truck gardening—sought to buy a small farm in the Bangor–Brewer area. When they spotted the little farm at the curve on the road in Holden, they were transfixed, much as my dad had been. Interestingly, they were a Black family, the Paines, whose ancestors had migrated through the Northeast in the 1860s to Canada and now, in a reversal of that movement, were anticipating a more appealing life in Maine. As it turned out, my parents were extraordinarily pleased that a deserving family might benefit from the land they had so cherished.

My dad, perhaps for sentimental reasons, retained a small woodlot, at best an acre or two, at the edge of the farm, and on subsequent occasions our entire family would picnic there under the birches. During summers in our preteen years, my brothers and I would venture out to the property, splash about in the swimming hole in the nearby stream, and deliver some used clothing or a gift of Mom's fruit cake to the Black family.

There were few Blacks in Maine at that time and the Paines were the only such family in the town. The produce from their gardens would become renowned throughout that region for decades.

The morning after Labor Day in 1931 was a moment of intense frenzy for the children on the hilltop. It was the first day of school, and Lorraine had spent the last weeks imagining the Excelsior School, her classmates, and her teacher. She was mature for eight, one year ahead in class for her age group, and eager to take brother Bobby's hand and join the three eldest Dougherty children in the walk down Chamberlain Street.

The Excelsior was the archetype of the two-story wooden school. Built in the 1880s, it housed grades primary (known as kindergarten today) through six. Except for the primary grade, two classes occupied each large classroom, its teacher responsible for two grades with diverse ability levels. Unlike some school systems of its time which typically employed mostly single women, the teachers at Excelsior had husbands and families, possibly reflecting a stable and unchanging social climate in the town.

Lorraine was assigned to grade four, Mrs. Folsom's room. As she climbed to the second floor, she became aware of the generations that had negotiated that staircase, cupping the treads with their repeated footsteps to the point where the town ceased to repaint them. At recess on that first day of class, Lorraine met Charlotte Anderson and Lita Murphy, who'd be friends through high school and beyond. All of the classrooms at Excelsior contained a mixture of town children along with a sprinkling of young people from the nearby countryside. School luncheon programs were still well in the future and the majority of students walked home for their midday meal, returning quickly before the one o'clock bell. The country children gathered in the school's basement to consume sandwiches wrapped in wax paper and drink milk from mayonnaise or jelly jars brought from home.

Our mother long complained about the school culture that sent small children home midway through the instructional period, when an in-school luncheon program would benefit both students and faculty. She was also concerned that many youngsters lacked adequate food at home and that schools should assume at least a partial obligation to feed them—it was, after all, the years of the economic depression, and many homes lacked a breadwinner. By the late 1930s, government programs had been introduced to provide some students with a warm lunch, but these plans were available largely to students bused to school, country children. Mother, I'm sure, didn't resent country kids obtaining a free lunch (she was doubly concerned with those same youngsters having to store their food without refrigeration), "But why," she wondered, "didn't they go all the way?" It would no doubt be an invaluable favor not only to the students' families but to the entire community. She was, of course, ahead of her time.

A bell would ring at three thirty, and the students would begin their homeward trek. Sometimes going home would be delayed so that the principal (also Mrs. Folsom) could remind them to bring in their "milk money" or money for a savings program or, as it happened, pennies to help save the USS *Constitution*—Old Ironsides—slowly deteriorating at a pier in Boston. Before leaving the schoolyard, Lorraine would collect her little brother, Bobby, and as in the morning, the hilltop gang would walk homeward together.

Once home, Lorraine was often pressed into service helping Mom care for me and my slightly older brother, Floyd. 'Rainey (or 'Rain, as I generally called her) and I developed a solid bond from my earliest time. She even claimed in later life that she'd contested my mother as to whose baby I was! In any event, I basked in the love of both. Traditions, developed over centuries, well established the role of older females as caregivers to younger children. Lorraine's dilemma as the oldest girl was that she was followed by a string of male siblings—five to be exact. The situation was bound to build up resentment, as it had between our mother and hers, though I didn't learn of 'Rainey's displeasure until many years later. Our dad, no doubt, had much to do with maintaining a peaceable household. He held the respect and love of both wife and daughter. He understood the predicament of both women, and he frequently stepped in to help with the children or to prepare meals. (My mother acknowledged him to be "the best cook in the family.") All children in our family would eventually have duties or chores to perform. The sooner you did your work, the sooner you'd be allowed to dip into the peanut butter and marshmallow fluff. Often, we'd only need to change our clothes before getting the treats.

I was a babe in arms that first winter on Chamberlain Street. The second floor of our house had been given temporary partitions: our parents' bedroom, Lorraine's bedroom, the boys' bedroom (more dormitory than room), and a post-nursery. My crib was in my parents' room. I had pushed Floyd out of that favored position to the post-nursery, where Lorraine would keep an eye on him. As we matured we would be shuffled around. I would then join Floyd in what became the second boys' room. We retained our cribs, though the sides were removed, and we felt we'd been socially elevated. Downstairs had the usual divisions of living room, dining room, and kitchen. The kitchen was spacious, and nearly every activity took place there. The dining room, ostensibly for serving meals, became a utilitarian space: a bedroom for Grandpa if he chose to sleep in the house, a study with its Stickley desk for Lorraine, and a sewing room for mother with her

Singer machine hidden behind the door. When illnesses would occur, the dining room was the sick bay. Our house presented tight quarters at times, yet we were a happy family, content with our fortune of a new home.

Grandpa Alex was enchanted with his new arrangements. He exalted in being close to the family without burdening a crowded, small home. The family, too, enjoyed gazing out on the cottage, seeing smoke curling into the cool morning air, and knowing everything was well. At times, he'd invite the older children to join him for breakfast which he'd cook woods style on the little stove. Despite a whirlwind of material considerations during the construction, Alex, whom the children usually called "Papa," attended Mass at Saint Joseph's Church nearly every day. He'd walk to church at seven, share in the Holy Communion, and not break his fast till he sat down with the family at eight-thirty. Over time he became friendly with the young priest, Father Thomas Moriarty.

Father Moriarty was the sole pastor of the parish, which had been formed only a few years earlier. This was the priest's second assignment, having previously served at a tiny, remote church in Woodland, Maine. His parishioners in Woodland were a mixture of Wabanaki Indians and French–Canadian families. It was logging country where a French patois predominated, and Moriarty quickly picked up the language. Consequently, he and Papa Landry hit it off readily.

That autumn of 1931 saw Dad and Grandpa buttoning up the house for an anticipated cold winter. Positioned in an open field without the shelter of trees, the new house would be constantly assaulted by winds swooping in from the north and east. They built banking boards, placing them at an angle against the foundation, to further insulate the house from the weather. (The use of banking boards was a northern Maine custom for years but was largely abandoned in the latter half of the twentieth century, when central heating and cheap fuel prices became the norm.) Around the shed, screens were lifted and replaced with solid wood panels. On the house itself, storm windows and doors replaced the screens of summer. These jobs were labor intensive, requiring the men to climb ladders as they balanced heavy loads. It was a ritualistic event that indelibly marked the change in seasons. Considering that my father had a prosthesis, their accomplishment was all the more remarkable.

Their work was finished just before Thanksgiving, and the two rode out to Corinth in the Essex, finding an old acquaintance who raised turkeys from whom they selected a bird for the table. They waited patiently as they heard the commotion of the victim protesting its demise, paid the farmer, and took a dressed fowl home. After returning from early Mass on Thanksgiving morning, Grandpa joined Mom in preparing his bread stuffing à la Canadienne, with copious quantities of sausage, onions, and garlic. In typical fashion, Dad would then take over the cooking duties. He would singe the turkey in the parlor stove to remove feathery debris, stuff and sew up the bird's cavity, and place it in the oven of the Glenwood stove at a moderately high heat. "It'll be ready in just five hours," he predicted.

Mom and Dad loved traditions and, once in place, they were followed—even if slightly frivolous—down through the years. It became customary for my parents to equally share both the joys and burdens of the holidays.

At the approach of Christmas, 'Rainey and Bobby "borrowed" Dad's hatchet, announcing they were going to produce the family's tree. Pulling a sleek "Flyer" sled with its red runners, they headed for Doughertys' Woods. For good measure, Grandpa decided to accompany the two little woodsmen. The woods, a quarter of a mile away, was a microcosm of Maine's forest; dominated by aged pines of considerable height, it was a virtual botanical garden of pointed firs, graceful hemlocks, birches, poplars and, in a few wet meadows, gnarly old red cedars. In summer, dairy cows wandered there freely, their cloven hooves creating a pattern of shallow trenches appearing as though made by a human landscaper. In winter, the dark conifers stood in contrast to the snow-covered forest floor, like a child's wonderland. Here and there wild winter berries and low shrubs punched through the snow. While snow covered the cow paths, they still stood out, marking the walking trails.

Finding a copse of balsam firs, Grandpa demonstrated how, by rubbing the twigs between their fingers, they could identify the sweet smelling "Christmas" tree. The children examined a number of specimens before 'Rainie proclaimed she'd found the "perfect tree," one with symmetrical branches and standing a foot above her head. Grandpa nodded his approval and proceeded to show how, by alternating vertical and horizontal whacks with the hatchet, to bring the tree down. With the tree felled and tied to the sled, the trio jauntily set out for home.

Christmastime brought out its own set of customs: simple decorations that spoke of the innocence of the season, yet a warm atmosphere in and out of the house that was welcoming and joyful. My father loved lining up the children to sing a little ditty called "Kris Kringle Day is Coming!" Our parents would join in the singing, and in the evening, we'd be given hot chocolate or Ovaltine. Our anticipation of Saint Nicholas was palpable.

I may have been in a bassinet or lying in a playpen struggling to sit up, but I was most likely conscious of a festive atmosphere.

"The bungalow home" at 159 Chamberlain Street.

CHAPTER 12

I was eleven months old—and my memory does not extend that far back—when we lost Grandfather Alex. As the story in our family went, Grandpa had worked himself into a heavy sweat one steamy summer day, "caught pneumonia" and quickly died. He had been "happy beyond words," my mother would tell us, having his son, daughter-in-law, and their children there in a home he'd helped build. He cherished having the grandchildren sit patiently on his doorstep as he whittled them a doll or a musical instrument, or seeing them run to his cottage to tell him supper was on the table. It all ended so abruptly.

My parents' prospects during these early years of the Great Depression mirrored those of many families across a wide spectrum of America. That they found the courage to build their home while experiencing partial unemployment was commendable. But it was becoming evident that a vast change in our national government was required to lift us out of an economic quagmire that seemed only to worsen month by month.

It was during these disconsolate times that my family became friendly with the little lady and retired school teacher, Lila Curtis, who lived across the way. Generations before, the Curtis house had been pulled by a team of draft horses to its present location from below the hill on Chamberlain Street. It was a classic New England cape with a moderately sized shingled barn that was, by our time, connected by a glassed-in ell. Miss Curtis had a decidedly green thumb, and her flower gardens, fruit trees, and shrubs were the envy of her neighbors—including my mother. Lila Curtis, whom some considered a "quiet, retired, old maid," was a lively conversationalist with my dad. She was a conservative, stalwart Republican and he a progressive, open-minded Democrat.

Some of my earliest memories were of Miss Curtis and my dad having polite conversations. They would bandy about the name Roosevelt, my father indicating whoever possessed that name could lead us out of our troubles, Miss Curtis adamant that "that Roosevelt is a communist and a socialist, and he's going to lead us to ruin!" I hadn't any basic knowledge of what was going on, but I knew that Roosevelt was at the center of it!

By this time, the man in the conversation had been elected President of the United States. "A good thing," my mother asserted. "Things couldn't get much worse." There were things even a child could not help but observe, like destitute men who'd walk up our street looking for a handout, some well-dressed, their frayed and soiled clothing betraying their misfortune. There were tar-papered shacks outside of town where families, forced out of their homes, were hunkered down. They were trespassers—refugees within their own country.

Mr. Roosevelt was reelected in 1936, and my parents acknowledged that things were indeed getting better. My father had finally secured a full time position with the McLaughlin Company in Bangor, a retailer of appliances and assorted automotive equipment. In many aspects, it was work similar to that he'd had with the Maytag Company, and he told Mom, "Ruth, we can now look forward to the years ahead, instead of just holding our own." But there would be rough spots along the way, and the country would not fully regain its economic health until the war years.

Childhood memories are clouded by happenings that are partially fact, sometimes distorted by later experience, compounded by memories of others, or grown out of family legend. Science also may dispute as to when long-term recall first takes place. One of my earliest and more distinct memories was that of mischievously bathing one of my sister Lorraine's antique German dolls and incurring her wrath. I had engaged the help of my little brother Howard, then a toddler, in the nefarious deed, and our crime resonated within the family for years. By extrapolating that event with my brother's level of development, I determined I was two and a half years of age. A more pervasive memory of my preschool years was that of new arrivals—Ruth Marie in 1934, and Patricia in 1936. These additional siblings rounded out the family, finally, at eight children, with fourteen years between oldest and youngest.

On the Tuesday after Labor Day in 1936, I was roused early by an older brother, dressed in knickers and a shirt with aviation wings embroidered on its pocket, and given my breakfast. I was going to school for the first time. and most of my siblings would be setting out to rejoin their respective classes. The excitement that morning was tangible, and our voices at a fever pitch. "Make sure to hold your brother's hand," Mom instructed George Jr., four years my senior. "And don't forget to walk him home with you for lunch," she called, as we left the house on our walk down Chamberlain Street.

We had walked only as far as the Fords' house next door, when we were offered a ride to school. The Ford brothers, David and Jim, had acquired a Model A roadster with a convertible top and a back seat. They encouraged George Jr. to open the door and seat himself; we were to follow. When Junior touched the door handle, he received a mild shock from the low voltage battery. The Ford boys howled with laughter. The prank wiring was soon detached, however, and we all climbed aboard. We laughed, too, but not till we'd descended from the car.

Mrs. Farrington, only distantly related to Alice Farrington, was my sub-primary teacher. This beginning level was the rule throughout most of Maine, whereas much of our nation then, and even in more current times, did not offer this entry-level schooling. This was a full day program with an afternoon nap, unlike many contemporary primary or kindergarten classes which are half-day. 'Rain and Bobby had pre-schooled me in the alphabet and my numbers, and I was soon permitted to read *Dick and Jane* aloud to my classmates. I began to form friendships the first day, and before the week was out, I'd found my first girlfriend, Charlene Gallagher. I would badger my brother to let me stop at Charlene's house, right next to the school, where, when her mother signaled, we could dip into a bowl of chocolate-covered malt balls before continuing homeward.

Recess time was, like the classroom, every bit a learning center. It was where older boys taught us the fundamentals of life, girls, and sports. The school was surrounded by a gravel playground—no paving, no lawns. It was easily adapted to sports and games. In the spring, children would come to the schoolyard before classes began, the girls jumping rope to the tune of ageless rhyming ditties, the boys engaged in ferociously competitive games of marbles. At recess the children would pick up seamlessly from where they'd left off in the early hours.

The playing of marbles involved rules that evolved over generations. One version required the player(s) to assume a position with all four limbs on the ground and, from the circumference, knock his opponent's "glassies" (as we called them) out of the circle. It seemed that country boys were superior in this sport; their thumbs were trained to snap out the "shooter" marbles at a higher velocity and truer trajectory than we town boys. Their competitiveness on the playground seldom translated to success in the classroom, however.

It was in the second grade that I formed my friendship with Teddy Brown. Frederick Sewall Brown, whose father was a prominent banker and whose mother was president of the local DAR chapter, and I became inseparable friends throughout my elementary school days. As an only child, Teddy not only had his own bedroom but a playroom as well. Such arrangements were unthinkable luxuries to a boy who shared living and bedroom spaces with seven other siblings. Teddy's parents appreciated me and my family, and the two of us were treated equally. His parents were impressive people, even to a seven- or eight-year-old boy; his dad, always meticulously dressed in a three-piece suit and his mother in skirt and blouse, were the models of decorum. They were not stuffy or pretentious people, however, and I would learn a great deal from both of them.

Sewall Brown, Teddy's father, was a self-made man, in many respects like my dad. He'd had more formal school than my father, to be sure, but like my dad, he'd achieved by accepting opportunities and performing well. Unlike my father, Sewall Brown had deep roots in Bangor, and his social and business connections were most likely extensive. He was also a patriotic son of the community and as a member of the National Guard, had served on the Mexican border in 1916 ("Fruitlessly chasing Pancho Villa," he'd told us), and later, as a member of the Allied Expeditionary Force in France, returning home as a sergeant in the Army. Kind and thoughtful, he'd ask us meaningful questions about nature, religion, even politics, and listen attentively, his pipe clenched between his teeth and usually in need of lighting. He avoided giving us answers, as he was more interested in our adolescent thinking.

Like her husband, Dorothy Brown was from a well-respected Bangor family. I was occasionally invited to dine with the family, and from Mrs. Brown I learned social graces and manners, some far removed from those observed in our home. Yet she was never overly critical. As I remember, she did scold Teddy sometimes. (I guess that was her way of reaching me as well.) She possessed a high degree of interest in the arts and in furniture. From her I learned that—at least in their household—all the furnishings had a meaning and most a history. Dorothy Brown was more than the leader of the local Daughters of the American Revolution; her soul was in collecting the antiques of that period. At the Browns' eighteenth century summer cottage, which they'd lovingly restored on nearby Wiswell Hill, she relished showing Teddy and me the artifacts and crafts of that time. I was keenly interested, though I observed Teddy was only politely so.

Wiswell Hill was the terminus of a ridge of hills south of Holden. It had been settled in the early 1700s and was, with its splendid views toward the west and the Penobscot Valley, an appealing and safe place for frontier farmers of that period. Its attractiveness was not lost on more contemporary folks, and some of the farms on the hill had been gentrified, their owners commuting back to Bangor.

Not so, however, with Dick Hart. He'd been born on the hill, never venturing downhill until he was in his twenties. Teddy had discovered him and, being an only child, had established a bond with Dick in lieu of having a playmate his own age. In the 1930s Dick was in his fifties, though furrowed brow, black deeply sunk eyes, and wrinkled face—usually needing a shave—made him seem even older. The Hart farm, now ten acres, was a shadow of what it must have originally been. The Hart and Wiswell families had many times subdivided their acreage, and now Dick, with only hand tools, managed a one-cow farm, supporting himself and an aged mother. They maintained a moderately large barn, in addition to the house and the chicken coops, and Dick gave Teddy and me full run of the place. We discovered a world of early farm tools and implements, and the old farmer was always eager to explain and enlighten our knowledge of the previous centuries and farming in general.

On many Saturday mornings, a Silver Streak Pontiac driven by Mr. Brown would enter our drive to pick me up for some adventure. It might be a trip to an Indian reservation or it might be to an air show—the barnstorming variety at the time. My fondest memory was of attending the Woodsmen's Show when I was ten or twelve. Teddy was with us of course, but they'd also brought his cousin, Nancy Prescott. To me, Nancy, with moderately long, blond hair, dark eyes and prominent cheekbones, was stunningly attractive. I sat between her and Teddy, trying to view the musical performance in front of us. (The Woodsman Show was a traditional midwinter exhibit, largely of outdoor sports, with a variety show of music and logging that had some collective "woods" theme.) The lighting had dimmed and the lady on stage, with feathers and headband, had launched into "Indian Love Call," when a very soft hand found mine. It caught me unawares and it set off an unexpected response deep within me. Cupid's arrow had found me, even if just for a moment. For Teddy, the whole business of bringing his girl cousin was an annoyance, at the least.

I had many friends during my elementary school days. In addition to Teddy, there were Donald Schofield, Joby Collette, Edwin Roberts, Donnie Preble, and Johnny McClain. My friends were like connective tissue between my two worlds of home and school. At times, after school or on Saturday, we might go exploring along the Indian trail on the cliffs above the Penobscot, searching for arrowheads. At other times, particularly on rainy afternoons, we'd play board games or just hang out, bragging about some distant relative who'd achieved renown. If the friend lived in one of those old, Victorian homes on Main Street with lots of cubbyholes and a barn, we'd engage in hide-and-seek. Our game—alternately quiet and boisterously loud—would end with shouts of "Ollie, ollie, enphary," which translated somehow into the game's ending, "You're home free." Frequently, that call would coincide with a parent's, "Your friends need to go home, now."

My playmates' parents were heedful of my wellbeing and behavior, as much as my own were. It led to a protected life with an abundance of sunshine and laughter, the cares of a troubled world mostly removed. But the reality of that world could never be far away. It would descend upon us most oppressively when we experienced the loss of a young classmate.

Donald Schofield lived just off my homeward route, and I'd often stop by his house. Donald had an interesting, almost adult face, and his hair was slicked straight back. He seemed to have a constant smile. His parents were extraordinarily pleasant and solicitous of our friendship with their son. As it turned out, the Schofield boy had rheumatic fever and would succumb only a year or two later. (A heart valve disorder, rheumatic fever has now become a rare childhood disease, thanks to antibiotics that treat strep throat, one of its causations.) His parents had gently messaged our parents that young Donald had a terminal condition and, though we were grieved, we were accepting of his passing.

When Joby Collette died it was much different. A ruggedly built boy with broad forehead and dark, curly hair, he often wore a black wool sweater, presumably knit by his mother. (I remember being envious of that sweater.) His family lived in a comfortable, refined home on North Main Street, a broad lawn reaching back to an open-porch Dutch-gabled house, birthplace of General, then Governor Joshua Chamberlain. The Collettes had an equally dignified summer place on Green Lake, some fifteen miles east, off the Bar Harbor Road. It was there at the lake, in the aftermath of a violent lightning strike, that Joby perished, his family unable to reach him on the second floor when the structure was engulfed in a mass of flames.

In subsequent years, I would occasionally encounter his older sister on the street, hoping to express my sorrow, but she would turn away. It was a catastrophic loss for the family. It was a tragic and deeply felt loss for his classmates.

The quality of teaching at the Excelsior was perhaps above average, with a notable, frequent appearance of the town's superintendent of schools. There was an emphasis on reading for the students, and our teachers read adventurous tales to us almost daily. They also read passages from the Bible. (Our schools were not totally separate from religion, then.) I loved the line from Psalm XXIII: "He maketh me to lie down in green pastures...."

Culturally, the Excelsior could not offer what schools in larger towns or metropolitan areas might provide. Ours did produce a credible *Mikado*, sung and acted by the upper classes, to the enjoyment of us younger students. Performed during school hours, there were no doting parents in evidence, none to hear Dicky-bird sing, "Oh, willow, tit willow, tit willow!" If we had a teacher in the visual arts, I don't remember, but we had a fine music teacher, Eleanor Smith, whose instructions in the elements of music led to a lifetime enjoyment of classical and other musical forms. I also recall Mrs. Smith's use of color—chartreuse and purple—so unlike most of our teachers whose attire set a monotonously dull tone. I'm sure I wasn't interested in fashions, but I did have a deep sense of color, which I attributed to my father and grandfather.

Childhood illnesses were a constant in our elementary school years, especially during the late winter and early spring. Measles was the most prominent of these illnesses, but epidemics of scarlet fever, mumps, and other communicable diseases were common. Vaccinations for smallpox—on the upper arm for boys and the upper thigh for girls, generally—had become the norm throughout most of the civilized world by the 1930s. We received our inoculations en masse at the Excelsior School, a full class each day. Vaccines for the more common childhood diseases, however, were still quite a few years away. When the latter illnesses invaded our household, they provided an opportunity for my mother to exhibit her natural skills for nursing and would rectify, at least for the moment, her disappointment about a career she'd been denied. Our dining room became a nursing ward for several sick children at a time, its proximity to the kitchen an advantage. When my father returned home in the early evening, he'd ask my mother, "So, how are our little patients doing?" I recall few doctor's visitations, largely because of our mother's capabilities.

It was an austere time for my family. Our parents could ill afford luxuries for themselves or for us children. Good fortune had shone briefly, however, when they'd been given an upright Baldwin piano a few years previously. "It was a fine instrument," my mother would later say, and it stood for several years in our moderately-sized living room. Its fate was to be handed over to another family, as it could not be accommodated when the interior of the house was finished amid subsequent renovations.

I recall the morning Mr. Booker, whose daughter was in my grade school class, backed his truck up to our front door, and with the help of several friends and my dad, hoisted and pushed the instrument aboard. My mother stood watching, her face grim, her lips silent.

"I really didn't have the talent," she later rationalized, though nobody believed her.

By the end of April, with the harshness of winter and illnesses abating, the grace of spring and the promise of summer were in the air. The school yard again echoed with young voices. Boys rushed home to fly their kites and play baseball, and the girls mounted their bicycles for a group ride past their purported boyfriends' houses. When the latter situation involved me, I ran blushingly to my "secret" hiding place under the eaves to evade the attention. I didn't truly mind the admiration of females as much as I resented the family's teasing that would follow. Yet, it was all part of springtime, marking the change of seasons, and the changes taking place within our bodies and in our environment.

CHAPTER 13

Some older folks in Maine say there are but two seasons in our region, the Fourth of July and winter! To the young in my time, summer was when Mom took us to Shiro's shoe store to buy new Keds sneakers, with high tops and, like Henry Ford's cars and trucks, always black. This would occur around Memorial Day and we would shed our knickers and don short pants, which most likely were hand-me-downs from an older sibling. No matter the date, this was the start of summer.

Summer would be much about play and doing things you'd laid aside because of school or the absence of time for dalliance. On the southeastern side of the house, a large field extended toward Eastern Avenue. This was our playing field, rotating from season to season, now beckoning us to bring out our bats, gloves, and baseballs. On the opposite side, between our house and that of the Fords, a long strip of field held a profusion of wildflowers, strawberries, and other edibles. Early in the spring, before they'd blossom with bright, yellow flowers, we would pick the dandelions. Their tender leaves gave us a welcome green addition to the table, well before our garden could be productive. By the first of June, wild strawberries were in abundance and, before we gathered to play, we were required to pick a full cup of the delectable fruit. There was no valid comparison in taste to those edible gifts of nature.

Our baseball games would get underway in mid-afternoon, mostly among the younger boys. As the afternoon progressed, the older boys would join in, having finished their chores and other obligations. The lineup for both teams was in constant flux, as one boy was called home and another would arrive on the field. I loved baseball—and sports in general— but I'd frequently steal away or not readily join in so that I might, instead, resort to my hideaway and read.

My "secret spot" was located above the staircase landing which, for unknown reasons, had never been boarded in. It was an ideal spot for a young boy, its shoulder wall under the eaves restricting entry to older and bigger children. There I assembled my books, many of them gifts from Teddy Brown's family, and assorted other possessions. The Browns had introduced me to the Hardy Boys, but also to Kenneth Robert's *Arundel*. Over the next few years, I'd devoured all of Roberts's novels. When I'd go "missing" everyone knew where to find me. When my brothers needed another player to even up the team, they would come after me, often to my mother's encouragement that "he needs some sunshine and fresh air."

Though summer had astronomically begun some two weeks earlier, the Fourth of July was undoubtedly the beginning of hot weather, and of a renewed faith that our gardens would grow more rapidly and lake water would be warm enough for swimming. In our neighborhood on Chamberlain Street, the day began with a resounding explosion that echoed off the houses, only to be followed by continuous detonations through the morning or until the boys (of all ages) had exhausted their munitions. Our mother cautioned us repeatedly about the danger of fireworks and we were hence armed with low-caliber firecrackers and caps (to be hammered). Mother's warnings would, regrettably, be validated in the newspaper the following morning with reports of lost fingers and limbs.

July Fourth was my birthday, and I usually received a one-dollar bill from Dad, fresh from the bank. One dollar was the equivalent to several hours of wages for a working man at that time. It made me feel...well... as rich as Rockefeller, and I'd store it away among my treasures. Dinner, at midday, would feature a poached Atlantic salmon, fresh from one of Maine's rivers, and early peas, raised and picked that morning from our garden. The peas were enhanced with Mom's traditional cream-and-egg sauce. Being my birthday, I usually requested and received my favorite cake, gingerbread with buttercream frosting. As evening approached, we would all, somehow, load into the car and go for ice cream cones. Afterward, we'd attend the fireworks display at the Athletic Field which, my father would insist, was being performed to celebrate my big day. I chose to believe him.

One of the aspects of a Maine summer is its pleasantly cool, low-humidity weather. We grew up in a time before homes were mechanically cooled with air conditioning. Our house on the hilltop usually benefitted from a constant breeze throughout most of the summer. The temperatures inland, unlike those near the coast, can soar in late July and August, and ninety,-degree days and brief hot spells were not uncommon. When, on those nights, our rooms upstairs were uncomfortable, we would move *en famille* to the front lawn. There were no streetlights then and the residual light from the community was of such low density that we could see the heavens as never before. In late summer the aurora borealis, or northern lights, with its shimmering bands of incandescence, was magical. My parents and older brother Bobby would tell us about the stars and the constellations and the astrological figures superimposed there. I would awake in the morning mysteriously in my bed, brother Bobby having transported me there as I slumbered.

There was mostly peace—save for China—throughout the world in the fall of 1937. There were occasional disruptions in the quietude in our country: dust storms in the Midwest and gangsters, born out of a now discredited Prohibition experiment, operating in various parts of the nation. But New England in general, and Maine in particular, seemed to have been backwaters to this violence. Bangor, perched on the banks on the Penobscot River in Eastern Maine, 1200 miles east of Chicago, 500 miles north of New York City, and some five hours north of Boston, was effectively beyond the rough-and-tumble vibrations in those parts. Happenings beyond Boston were systematically back-paged by the *Bangor Daily News*, weighted someplace between "news from other places" and the market prices for local eggs and Maine potatoes, now being picked in Aroostook County. It was quiet, and Maine folks liked it that way. This tranquility was about to jarringly change.

Our first story had its beginnings in the Midwest. Alfred Brady, a farm boy, had been born on a small place in Brook, Indiana. He was soon—at age two—to suffer the first in a series of misfortunes, when his father died. His mother died when he was sixteen, having entered three additional marriages, leaving the youngster with increasingly unstable families. Downhearted and orphaned, Brady drifted into a life of wrong-doing. Several incarcerations only sharpened his anti-social tendencies. He engaged initially in petty crimes but, after meeting Rhuel James Dalhover, who shared Al's dismal upbringing, the two moved on to the more serious work of bank robberies and homicides.

By the winter of 1937, with Al Brady in the ascendancy, their "gang," never more than five participants, had committed nearly two hundred robberies, had three murders to their credit, and had firmly drawn the attention of the Federal Bureau of Investigation. Their specialty was bank robbery and their methodology simple. They would drive to a small hamlet or village in Indiana or Ohio, where there would be little or slim police protection, grab the cash quickly while maintaining an armed guard inside and outside the bank, and swiftly drive off. By early in 1937 they had nearly exhausted targets in those two states, and, with the "feds" on to them, decided a change of venue was in order.

Facing stiff headwinds from local and state police forces, the FBI, and possibly rival gangs, they headed east, landing in Bridgeport, Connecticut. They lived quietly there for a period, establishing a routine where some of them accepted employment and odd jobs and others acquired girlfriends and a social life. They made several forays to replenish their cash flow and, during one of the heists, got into a running gun battle with a lone policeman. The gang decided in the aftermath of that encounter they needed more firepower. Through some connections with several shady types, they were able to obtain a well-used Thompson submachine gun. It was inoperative, needing a few simple parts and some appropriate ammunition. The fisherman who sold it to them, a rum-runner during Prohibition, assured them of its capabilities, as he'd used it himself in his moonlighting trades.

Their activities had again alerted the FBI, who'd lost track of the gang since their leaving the Midwest. The Brady bunch gathered—they'd been living scattered around Bridgeport—and Al persuaded them to move on, though no destination was initially considered. One of the members balked, as he had a heavy relationship ongoing. He was convinced to tell his sweetheart that he had "a business deal to contend with out of town." Three of them—Al Brady, Rhuel Dalhover, and Clarence Lee Shaffer—left

Bridgeport in their stolen, 1936 Buick with Ohio plates in early October. A fourth member, Charles Griseking, had been captured along the way and was back in Indiana awaiting trial.

Traveling US Route 1, the men, all in their early twenties, considered Providence, then Boston, and then Portland, where they elected to change to Route 2 and proceed to a town called Bangor. They joked among themselves, "Who the hell would ever look for us in *Bangor*?"

Driving through Carmel, on the outskirts of Bangor, the men pulled into a tourist site called "Auto Rest" that offered a small collection of separate cabins and decided to hole up there. A middle-aged woman, who with her husband owned and managed the place, led them to a solitary cabin somewhat away from the other units. They paid her cash for a week's stay and asked for a deck of cards. To their question of eating dinner, she said, "Everything's closed out *he-yar*. You'll probably do better in *Ban-gor*, though some *says* the Turn Inn might be open, but they do more in booze than food. *Ban-gor* is your best bet, they got everything."

When the gang visited Bangor the next morning, one of them affirmed, "Yeah, they got everything here. Banks, big banks, *lotta* people and dogs though!" They motored around the downtown area and returned to where they'd started at the intersections of Hammond, State, and Main Streets. They found an eating spot, sat down in a rear booth, and ordered pork chops with peas and mashed potatoes. The men were relaxed, dove eagerly into their food, and struck up easy banter with their waitress.

"So, you're going huntin'? Real huntin' doesn't start 'round here till after Armistice Day. But you can bird hunt with a shotgun. My husband's going out partridge huntin' Columbus Day, it's a holiday *he-yar*." When the men asked about a gun shop, she signaled a direction around the corner. "Dakin's, it's right *th-ar*."

The following day they revisited the town, touring a few more streets. By mid-afternoon, both thirsty and hungry, at the urging of one of the locals, they parked in Haymarket Square and strode into the Narragansett Spa. On the bartender's recommendation, they each had a couple of "'Gansetts" and several hot dogs with sauerkraut. They went off in a corner and talked. "Gotta go visit Dakin's," Al said. "Shaffer, you go in. Case the joint a little. If it feels right, order the parts for the Tommy gun. Order some other stuff, like the ammo, too. We don't want to return till the stuff's on their counter, wrapped and ready for pickup!"

They left the spa, drove up to Main Street, down Main past shoppers entering and exiting Freese's Department Store and a multitude of ladies' clothing and shoe shops, to a spot nearby where they'd had lunch the previous day. Shaffer got out of the Buick, walked around the corner and entered Dakin's Sporting Goods Store on Broad Street. He glanced at several shotguns and picked up a lever-action 30-aught rifle, a renowned hunting gun in Maine. A clerk acknowledged his choice with an affirmative smile but returned to talk to another customer. Shaffer noted another clerk behind the counter finishing up some paperwork. Before Shaffer could introduce himself with some fictitious name, the clerk offered his hand and said, "I'm Shep. How can I help you?"

Shaffer discussed several items the gang was looking for initially, not the submachine gun parts. It was imperative that the goods be assembled on a given date, he added, as they would be traveling some distance from out of town. After the clerk assured them that their source could meet their request without questions, Shaffer asked if that included "parts for a Thompson?"

"Oh, yes," said Shep, "'cause we order stuff for all the police departments."

Seeing Shep's quizzical looks, Shaffer announced it was for "a fisherman friend in Massachusetts, who uses the weapon to ward off lobster poachers."

A date was set for the pickup and, as it would coincide with Columbus Day, Shep assured his customer that Dakin's was open every day but Sunday, and his goods would be "here on the counter." Shaffer was scarcely out of the door when Shep set down with his superior and said, "I think we need to alert the cops; what do you think?"

The chief of the Bangor Police Department, on hearing about the stranger from out-of-town who ordered parts for a Thompson submachine gun, put in a call to the Boston office of the FBI. Their response was not long in coming: "You may have someone important to us—someone who's a member of a gang from Indiana—keep under surveillance, if possible—we'll send you an agent."

Like a Greek tragedy, the *dramatis personae* were in place, the plot well-established, a calamity about to ensue. Agent Walsh, from the

FBI's Boston office, appeared over the weekend. He was joined by the heads of Maine State Police, the Bangor Police Department, and on Monday, an additional team of federal agents—"G-men" as they were popularly known.

Brady and his cohorts continued coming into town, but doing so quietly and away from downtown. As the Auto Rest owners would later attest, the "boys" were very peaceful, the only noises heard were when somebody won a big hand of poker. And, to an extent, they were boys, Al, at twenty-six, being the oldest.

By Monday, October 11th, Rhuel Dalhover was grumbling that if they stayed around much longer, they'd be "running out of the green stuff." He added that they shouldn't pay any more rent.

"Jesus, Jim," as Brady usually called Dalhover. "You want the lady to call the cops on me?" He assured him that they'd be leaving Wednesday morning at the latest.

Columbus Day fell on Tuesday, October 12, 1937. Maine had been part of Massachusetts until 1820, and like its sister state, observed that day as a holiday, though many of the principal stores in Bangor would remain open for business to serve a community largely on holiday. Shep regretted having to work on a day most folks had off, but he knew he'd be on stage— somehow—for a little bit of drama. He'd appeased his wife, who had the day off, by consenting to take her to lunch. He concluded, as he opened the sales counter, it would be a long morning.

It would be an exciting day for Al Brady and his friends. The third and fateful act was unfolding, as Al told Shaffer and Dalhover, "Throw your stuff into the trunk before we go; we might have to leave in a hurry." Their plan had been well-rehearsed. They'd drive to downtown Bangor, have breakfast at a joint they all liked, reposition their car in front of Brockway's Floral Shop and, with Al and Dalhover remaining in the Buick, Shaffer would enter the store and conduct his business.

As he got out of the car, Clarence Shaffer patted his chest, where a loaded revolver lay stashed under his jacket. He smiled at Al as he wheeled about heading to Dakin's Sporting Goods Store. "I'm going in behind you, if there's any trouble!" Brady promised. It was eerily quiet, even for a holiday, like an Edward Hopper painting of Main Street.

With advance notice of several days, a major contingent of law enforcement officers had assembled: local police officers as well as state police and federal agents. A cordon was established by the officers in all the stores surrounding Dakin's, on both ground floor and above. A number of federal agents, all sharpshooters, were stationed on rooftops, their weapons trained on the sporting goods store and the adjacent area.

There has never been a satisfactory explanation of what initiated the commotion, but Agent Walsh, out of nervousness or impatience, fired upon Shaffer, who'd barely come through the doorway. The gangster responded quickly, with at least one shot hitting Walsh, and fled out to the sidewalk. Hearing the gunfire, Al Brady threw open the door of the Buick and downtown Bangor erupted in gunfire. As Shaffer stumbled in the direction of the car, he was hit repeatedly and fell in the street. Brady was able to get well out of the car but was knocked to the pavement of Central Street by a fusillade of bullets. Dalhover, possibly because of fright, never emerged from the back seat of the Buick and was gravely wounded in the thunderous crossfire.

The massacre was over in a few minutes. The incident and the questions it raised have lingered for decades. Bangor lost an innocence that day, possibly one it never had. We learned from that, and from other events to come, that though we were geographically remote from much of the nation, we were forever part-and-parcel of its fabric, for good or for evil.

Columbus Day was a day off from school as well, and we'd looked forward to it. Older boys might go bird hunting with their dads. My brothers Floyd and Howard and I gathered with three or four friends and engaged in a wide-ranging game of "cowboy and Indians." It was one of those sublimely beautiful fall days, the windows and doors of our houses open to the pleasant atmosphere, when a voice from the Fords' house next door hollered over, "Turn on your radio!" (That was part of our "news alert" system.)

The news of the violence in Bangor's downtown, leaving two dead gangsters lying in the street, and another wounded but captured, was an astounding event—right here in River City! It was frightfully exciting to six- and seven-year-old boys. Our games after lunch morphed into cops and robbers. Forget about the Indians! None of us wanted to be the robbers, however.

New Englanders are often spared the violence of weather extremes and geological events that visit much of our country. To be sure, the region receives its share of cold and blizzards in the winter, but major disasters such as tornadoes in the Midwest and the South, vast flooding along the Mississippi, and hurricanes along the South Atlantic seaboard rarely occur in Maine. The year 1938 proved to be different.

The weather predictions for New England on Wednesday, September 21st, were for periods of rain continuing for several days. The news on that date was mostly political. In Boston's mayoral race, James Michael Curley, the hope of the Irish, would be the candidate for the rapidly rising blue-collar Catholic liberals and Leverett Saltonstall, the standard bearer for the blue-bloods of the North Shore and Beacon Hill, would be the Republican candidate for the reelection to the Senate. In Maine, Lewis Barrows would likely succeed himself as governor, having won his primary. In Bangor, the Community Chest would launch its fundraising on this day, with Mrs. Gordon Briggs of the Junior League leading its presidential solicitation. New Englanders are much at home with rainy weather, and this seemed just another wet episode.

The ferocity of this storm system, with recorded winds as high as a hundred miles per hour, deceived the weather services with both its power and its initial landing north and east of Long Island, over Block Island, and into Narragansett Bay. The winds and water surges spread death and destruction throughout Southern New England. Maine and New Hampshire would get hit later in the day with wind gusts of over a hundred miles per hour and torrential rains, sending onrushing waters crashing into riverside villages and obliterating dams and bridges.

My father had gone to work earlier that day. As news of the havoc in Providence and Boston became evident and as the fury of the storm increased locally, he'd decided to return home. The waters under the bridge were already raging and, as he crossed to the Brewer side, he watched as the swift flooding snagged piles of lumber and sent them cascading down river.

We dined that night under a flickering kerosene lantern, feeling secure in our bungalow, even as the house vibrated constantly, and Mom put towels at the bottom of the doors to keep the wind-driven water from penetrating the house.

The 1938 Storm caused 657 deaths and left a broad swath of demolishment. Its destructive effects were felt as much inland, in the hills and mountains of New Hampshire, as on the coast. As late as the 1960s, after having acquired some wooded acreage in Sanbornton, New Hampshire, I discovered a moss-covered "regiment" of what must have been pristine, gigantic pines, downed by winds that crossed the shoreline some hundred miles away. The rarity of a windstorm of such magnitude sent historians back to the Colonial Hurricane, which had devastated parts of Virginia, New York, and New England some three hundred years earlier.

As the flood waters subsided in the Northeast, people took note of events unfolding in Europe. In Italy, Benito Mussolini's regime had created a Fascist government. In Germany a well-established dictatorship under Adolf Hitler was rearming and had annexed Austria. And in Spain, General Francisco Franco was conducting a civil war against a constituted republic. These events had set Europeans—and much of the world—on edge.

In the midst of this anxiety, a radio drama, broadcast to the American public on the Eve of Halloween, produced an unintended fright and near panic among listeners, most of whom had dialed in to the broadcast late. Narrated by the actor Orson Wells, the *War of the Worlds* was an imaginative work by the British author, H.G. Wells (unrelated to Orson), and its theme of a fictional Martian invasion had been alluded to before the program began.

Like most listeners on the East Coast, we had dialed in late. "Tanks are rolling in the streets of New York City. Crowds, miserably frightened, are fleeing, taking refuge in buildings off Times Square." We sat incredibly stunned, perplexed by the hysteria being described. We weren't alone. With a nervousness conditioned by a world in disruption, by an actor whose dramatic voice had no parallel or who better projected "reality," we were perfectly positioned for a big scare. Fortunately, the network became alerted to the impact Wells's presentation was having on the audience that evening, and a moment of explanation followed the performance. As children, we needed comforting and reassurance after "the invasion forces had retreated." Few of us might have imagined then that the fictional *War of the Worlds* was but a prelude to real war about to descend upon us in the following year.

The year 1939 proved to be a good one for our nation and a better one for my family. In the West, climatic conditions that had created the dust bowl had dramatically abated, along with improved farming methods and farm production, and prices had risen. Across the country, manufacturing was approaching pre-Depression levels, and household incomes were rising. Though it would take a major war to see America fully recover from the Depression, economic advancement was evident in every state and municipality, and in most households.

As Europe teetered on the verge of war, the Roosevelt administration initiated preliminary steps to prepare for the hostilities we ardently hoped to avoid. In Bangor, Dow Field of the Army Air Corps, was being carved out of farming country between Hammond and Union Streets and four thousand workers were receiving paychecks. Across the river in Brewer, a new city hall, courtesy of the federal government, was opening its door. On State Street, adjacent to the Athletic Field, a new city auditorium was rising. We watched from our house as masons and hod carriers erected the walls and cranes lifted into place the arc-shaped steel girders which supported and defined the roof's shape. It was exciting to watch, even from a distance, as riveters, silhouetted against the sky, hammered home the structural pieces. It was all part of a massive program to put Americans to work.

JJ McLaughlin Company, where my father worked, was a bustling small business. Dad was its one-man sales force, and standing among rows of gleaming electric ranges, refrigerators, and washers, he greeted the local housewives who saw the machines as a glamorous escape from wearisome household tasks—as well as status symbols. He and the owner, JJ, enjoyed a pleasant and friendly relationship, though Dad would sometimes comment that JJ "preferred reading the *Wall Street Journal* to selling washing machines." The McLaughlin Company did remarkably well in its business, particularly as it competed against a Sears, Roebuck store across the alley, which sold many of the same brands and lines of appliances. "People bought the idea of local service," Dad would say, "and a personal touch that Sears could not offer."

With heartening income prospects, my parents were in an expansive mood in the prewar years. The hurried move into the newly built house from the little farm in Holden had left much unfinished. "We'll start from the bottom up," my father announced. "I'll hire a small crew. They can finish the digging out in the basement and lay a concrete floor. We need to do all that, so that we can install the furnace and central heat." Few homes had the luxury of a central heating system at that time. At best, they might employ a furnace in their cellars that sent warm air through a large register that ostensibly heated the house. Parlors and kitchen stoves, however, were still more common.

The work my parents anticipated was laborious, requiring, as the Maine expression goes, "a weak mind but a strong back." The assembled crew— perhaps four in all—were certainly a rough, unpolished contingent. I took an interest in their work, however, passing the men glasses of cool water, and watching my father lay out elevations for the concrete deck. After the work was finished and the crew paid and departed, Dad remarked that they had done a reasonably good job for a "rough crew." Two of them, he said, had been incarcerated, one for violating the Mann Act. As my mother put it, sympathetically, they were simply troubled men.

Of course, I had to ask about the Mann Act, and I was told in clinical terms, it was about transporting a woman across a state line for immoral purposes. (*Who knew?* I must have thought. You can sure learn a lot watching a rough crew doing gritty work!) Everything turned out well and, as the concrete cured, the plumbers and steamfitters from Flagg & Sons were sending pipes up and about the house. We would finally have a warm and cozy home.

It was half-time at the Athletic Field in September of 1939, and the Brewer High School Witches were playing their archrivals, the Bangor Rams. We were alerted that the football game had become a pitched battle. Windy Work had scored for Bangor, and the Rams now led. I had walked to the field on State Street with my year-older brother, Floyd, who, before disappearing, shouted back to me that he was going to "jump the fence or sneak under it." He added, "If you don't want to follow me, you can go home!" I must have been in my righteous years, as I declined to follow and stood near the gate as the Brewer squad came jogging out, looking game but fatigued. The team was headed for the Brown (Holyoke) family's barn a few yards distant, to rest and recover before the second half commenced. The town's sports field, subtly called the Athletic Field, had impressive playing grounds but no dressing rooms, lockers, or other facilities. I decided to follow the team, observing as I ran, that other lads were jogging along with me.

I was slightly in awe of high school boys who played football, their black, heavily cleated shoes and stiff shoulder pads magnifying their brawniness. At home the talk was all about football (when it wasn't about boxing or baseball), and every youngster had his heroes: Tom Harmon of Michigan, the Fighting Irish of Notre Dame and its legendary coach, Knute Rockne.

The Brewer coach, Dana Dougherty, had just concluded his pep talk of "Let's get out there and do our job!" The team seemed reinvigorated and were reassembling in front of the barn, when Buddy Lyford, a friend of my oldest brother, Bobby, spotted me. Bud, the team's fullback, must have sensed my ticketless predicament, and he and five or six other players picked me up and, as if I were a wounded comrade, ran with me suspended back to the field, their cleats clattering on State Street's concrete pavement, and through the gate. I've long forgotten who won that day, though I've not ceased to remember the dramatic entry to my first game.

As we lived in close proximity to the field, football games were routine on Saturdays. We attended games at the Mary Snow Field in Bangor, as well. Win or lose, they were stimulating to us would-be football players. Coming home after the game was equally heady, as Mom baked all day on Saturdays, so, with expanded appetites and aroused senses, we anticipated the fresh rolls and loaves of yeast bread, the apple and mince pies, and the chocolate donuts. We would usually receive a roll or biscuit, hot from the oven, or a doughnut, just enough to check our impatience. The parade of baked goods, the product of a full day's work, was meant to last a week. It was a feast that, even when doled out frugally, would be exhausted by Wednesday.

It was during these same years that we younger siblings discovered religion, or perhaps religion discovered us. My parents were not antireligious though for a variety of reasons did not attend church. Coming from a Judaist family, my mother would have had a natural reluctance to accept another theology—that of Christianity. My father had a hesitancy, even as a youth, to follow his own father into the Catholic faith. With the inconvenience of a prosthesis (and the church's propensity for kneeling), he felt even less inclined to churchgoing. But our parents kept their counsel and encouraged our older siblings, and later the rest of us, to follow Grandpa Alex and attend Saint Joseph's Roman Catholic Church.

My curiosity about "church" had been aroused for some time. I pictured it as something like school where the parishioners dragged up folding chairs and the good father, standing in the center of the ring, told them imperious tales.

When the time arrived, my brothers Floyd and Howard, sisters Ruth Marie and Patricia, and I were rounded up and driven en masse in the back of "Uncle" Lou Dougherty's International truck to a christening at St. Joseph's. Father Moriarty dutifully dipped our foreheads in holy water and our sponsors (and godparents-to-be), Lou and Betty Dougherty, swore to renounce Satan in our names.

On subsequent Sundays, Howard and I watched as the older children from the hillside marched ahead of us downhill to church. "Hutch," as we more familiarly called him, and I would allow the others to disappear and then divert to the old brickyard meadow. We were still more comfortable in our disappearing heathen ways and, depending on the season, we'd roam about knocking down apples, damming up the brook, or catching pollywogs. Sometimes, Dick and Jack Tremble, brothers and fellow truants, would join us. There may be a paradise achieved through church, but our Eden, at that time, was there in the brickyard.

When the church services ended, and the others were walking back up the hill, we'd follow, arriving home in a jocular mood. Our capers ended when, asked about the "Lesson" on a given Sunday, we could only reply, "We just didn't get it!" And when Mom noticed, on repeated Sundays, that our shoes and pant cuffs were wet and muddy, we realized the jig was up.

By the time of my First Holy Communion, I had fully accepted going to Mass, enjoying the music, and the liturgy of the "stories." There was one exception, and that was Sunday school. Some of our friends, who were young Protestants, said they liked Sunday school—it was likely a substitute for church services. At Saint Joseph's, Father Moriarty had instituted a Sunday program wherein we had to return in midafternoon. This allowed him, as the parish's only priest, to better supervise our teachers and our catechism lessons. We felt it was an infringement on our playtime. Fortunately, Sunday school ceased during the summer. (Hallelujah!)

Father Thomas Moriarty, whom Grandfather Alex had befriended some years before, was the first priest assigned to Saint Joseph's, a former mission church of St. John's from across the river. Father Moriarty was a native of Holyoke, Massachusetts, and he'd been educated and attended seminary in the Bay State. From personal observations, as well as those of many others, he had a difficult personality. It may have contributed to his early assignment to the Portland (Maine) Diocese's far off Woodland parish. He could be alternately fiery and soft-spoken. From the altar he could dispel the notions some might have that they were better Catholics or more favored parishioners. He would rail against egocentrics and the self-centered, as he did against Fascists and Communists from abroad. He could also be self-deprecating; he loved telling amusing stories about his youth and swimming across the swift-flowing Connecticut River. He would at times punctuate his homilies with amusing foibles of human "beans." Father Moriarty was both a clerical institution and an enigma.

At home the refinishing and other improvements continued during the warmer months. When a second summer of construction approached, which would be more disruptive to family life, our parents hinted there was a surprise that awaited us. We had noted—with some wonderment—that Dad and Mom would leave for half a day, taking Patsy, then a toddler, with them. Some weeks later, they brought several of us along on one of these cryptic journeys. We packed into the Ford, taking along picnic baskets, and headed west through the town of Hermon, continuing up Mars Hill, where, by an old filling station with its shingled canopy, we turned on to a narrow country road. We drove another six or seven miles seeing small farms scattered on either side of the road, eventually dropping down a dirt drive that was more path than thoroughfare. We emerged in front of a classic, gabled summer cottage. The "camp," as Mainers call a cottage, was attractively painted a yellow tone with white trim and green sashes. A porch, which needed new screens, wound around two sides of the structure and was, no doubt, where the owners spent most of the summer.

Rather than answering our eager questions about where we were, Dad posed his own: "Would you like to spend the summer here?"

Unable to believe what we were hearing, we answered in chorus, "Can we really? We *love* this place!"

The *place* on the southwestern shore of Hermon Pond, was adjacent to the beach and, as there were only a few cottages in the distance, afforded great privacy. Despite its appeal on the exterior, it was a true Maine "camp" with no electricity, plumbing, or running water. It was primitive but charming, "with all the conveniences of a logging camp," my mother would later chuckle. The scenario was laid out: We younger children would come stay here after the Fourth of July with Mom. Dad would join us on weekends. The older siblings, Lorraine and Bobby, would remain in town, where they had summer jobs. If my mother had imaginings about the isolation and the obvious deprivations, she didn't let on.

"We've not had money to send you boys to a summer camp, as some of your friends' families have," Mom said, "so we hope you'll have fun here." I sensed a tinge of quiet in her voice, realizing she'd be giving up a newly remodeled kitchen for several months. Happily for us, we'd be allowed to invite a friend from time to time. "They can travel out here with your father for the weekend."

The summers at Hermon Pond were some of the happiest of our youth. When we weren't swimming off the shallow beach that fronted our camp, we'd take *Half Pint*, our rowboat, out for a cruise, fighting over who'd man the oars, or go fishing for white and yellow perch. We usually caught something, and we'd bring the catch ashore, clean it, and then present it proudly to Mom. It would be our supper.

We had no close neighbors or other nearby children, but we had open fields, the woods, and the pond. Mother allowed us free range for our play, and we'd romp and frolic about, exploring the woods and shoreline.

Walking back to the farm road, we discovered a farmhouse, its clapboards weathered—having never been painted—its window sashes lacking glazing, and its brick chimneys in desperate need of pointing. The house was the equivalent of a country store and postal office. Their offerings were limited—bread, milk, eggs, and the like, much of it produced on their farm. We'd vie for the privilege of going there periodically for the mail, newspapers, and assorted groceries. On one such trip, I crashed Floyd's bike returning home. I'd placed my shopping bag, heavily weighted with fresh milk, in the basket above the front wheel. I miscalculated; with the law of physics and my inexperience against me, I went into an uncontrolled skid as I descended the graveled slope and pitched over the handlebars. I was moderately bruised in the tumble, but worst of all, I had to endure my brother's scolding and taunts for the rest of the summer. Within the family, it was "Floyd's bike," though I was part owner as I'd helped him earn it on his magazine route. I was, therefore, not as contrite as I might have been.

On weekends, my parents would have their own guests—usually a couple—and we would be on our own best behavior. Sometimes, the two couples, the men in short-sleeved shirts, the ladies in summery blouses, would take *Half Pint* out for an early evening row. A few hundred yards offshore, my dad would lay the oars across the gunwales, and the men would light up their cigarettes while the women mixed and passed around cocktails. Sitting on the porch, we could hear their cheerful voices, happily echoing across the calm waters of Hermon Pond. On their return, we'd wade out to meet them, haul *Half Pint* ashore, and help the foursome from the boat. The sun would be setting as we filed onto the porch. After we'd been given a light supper, we helped Mom set the porch for a little dinner party and then climbed the stairs to our bedrooms. (We boys would be sleeping four to a room, having given up a bedroom to our guests.)

In a world otherwise comprised of continuous responsibilities, it was fascinating to see my parents exhibit their carefree personae, to laugh spontaneously, to watch them create a romantic evening from good food, good friends, and a small reserve of spirits.

The summer days we had Daddy with us were all too few. It was no doubt a struggle to work in town and commute to your family on weekends. I never knew my dad to take a vacation then or later, nor a day off, unless he was seriously ill. Paid vacations were a rare commodity for American workers, including those on salaries. On rare occasions, Dad would inveigle JJ to give him a long weekend, and we'd make the most of it. We'd play variations of baseball, where our dad would take his turn at bat—he could hit quite well—and one of us would run for him. At other times, he'd take out his tools and, with a minimum of effort, make us a small piece of art. We watched once with astonishment, as he swiftly sculpted canoe paddles, using nothing but a hatchet and sandpaper. (They were better-handling paddles than commercially produced ones.) To show our gratitude we'd troop off to the ledges rising behind the farmhouse store and gather blueberries—his favorite food—and Mom would serve up a blueberry concoction, a la crème, we'd all share later.

Periodically, Floyd, Hutch, and I would accompany Dad back to town for a day or two, where we'd tend and water gardens and lawns and, in Floyd's case, paint the fence, a task of which we were never envious. Hutch and I alternated at pushing the hand-powered lawn mower, and afterward, I would trim the hedge under the front window boxes—Mom insisted that, among the boys, only I had "the eye for the job." As a final chore, we would carefully edge the lawn where it met the gravel drive, giving it a touch of youthful perfection.

Dad would beam and say "Good work! I couldn't have done as well!" As we drove out Hammond Street returning to the pond, he would detour to the ice cream stand, a "double-decker" for our efforts.

Summer memories are usually crowded with sunshine and balminess, but I remember when skies darkened, rain swept in from across the water, and lightning flashed and exploded around our cottage. We'd move our games to the porch, change the ground rules, and continue seamlessly with our play. If wind and rain made the porch untenable, we'd flee into the house where we each had a diversion. Mine was reading upstairs. The past owners had left behind a trove of *Life* magazines, documenting weekly events since the magazine's initial publication in 1936. The stories and photography were first-class, and I acquired a valuable insight into a world beyond Maine. The stories illustrated such diverse subjects as John Steinbeck's California of the migrant dust bowl farmers, the architecture of Frank Lloyd Wright, the art and beauty of the Southwest and the rise of Fascism in Europe and the Far East. As an eight-year-old, I would ponder about the near-glorification of a Germany under Hitler, a puzzling "world order" being created in Russia, and the American Lincoln Brigade caught up in a civil war in Spain. The tactics employed in the latter conflict—aerial and mechanized warfare—were harbingers of what was to befall all of Europe.

One morning, returning from the farm store with Hutch, he noted several vivid red maple leaves, declaring, "They're out of place!" Their colors had, indeed, altered overnight. The morning had heated up, and it didn't seem plausible that the seasons were about to change. It was late August and, back in the cottage, Mom assured us that nature knew what it was doing, and that our time in camp was ending.

"Good things always end," she said almost cheerfully. "We'll all be happy when we're home. You'll have your new bedrooms, and I'll have my kitchen back!" I knew all that, but still felt somehow that the world was shifting out of balance.

CHAPTER 14

Europe, which had been in periodic jitters since the rise of German Nazism in the early thirties, was experiencing emotional overload by the end of the summer of 1939. Without firing a single piece of artillery, through threats and political manipulations, Germany had advanced its concept of *Lebensraum* (living room) to include Austria and Czechoslovakia's Sudeten region. Its sights had now turned eastward to Poland. France and England, on whom European security would ultimately fall, were unwilling or unable to counter Germany's aggression. The best these countries could do was diplomatically appease the Germans and assure the world of "peace in our time." Britain's Prime Minister Chamberlain added gratuitously, "If we have to fight, it must be on larger issues than [these]."

"No man is an island," the poet John Donne had penned three hundred years earlier, but "a piece of the Continent." If the bell tolls for the loss of one country, "it tolls for thee" as well. Winston Churchill, both a past and future prime minister of England, understood that connectedness. "Britain and France had to choose between war and dishonor. They chose dishonor. They will"—eventually—"have war."

The weather report was for a cloudy Friday, September 1st, but by noon it had cleared, and temperatures had risen. At Mom's suggestion, we moved to the lawn on the northwestern side of the house and sprawled out on the shady grass to await the lunch—probably tuna fish on Friday—that Mom was preparing. Across the field, Jim Ford came bursting (again) out of his house, visibly excited and literally screaming, "They did it, they invaded Poland! Now just wait till the French and British get him [Hitler]!"

Mom was leaving the kitchen, our sandwiches stacked on a tray. She heard Jim's dispatch and the news had no doubt alarmed and frightened her. Her reaction, "Those damn industrialists!" surprised me. I sensed this was a grievous moment, no matter who was at fault, and that the imbalanced world I feared had descended upon us.

The hostilities in Poland had set the rest of Europe—with a few exceptions—into a frenzy of war preparedness. In Britain, an expeditionary force was assembled and transported to assist the French and Belgians. France, still mindful of its losses in a war concluded only twenty years previously, called up its army, trusting that its Maginot Line of fortresses would protect it from the east and a marauding German military machine. Poland was soon overrun, its cities demolished, and an occupying army in control. And then the guns strangely went quiet, as the German dictator waited for a possible acquiescence of his conquest by the allies, France and Britain.

In America, we took pause in considering a war that might engulf much of the world. Our sympathies were certainly with the plight of the Polish people, but the region and Hitler's intent were a continent, an ocean, and at least six time zones from us. Our national purpose was to avoid European entanglements. Should we get involved? Sentiment in 1939 ran largely against doing so. "Isolationism" was the watchword of the moment and to oppose it was—at least politically—an invitation to anathema.

In our home we talked of the war unfolding in Europe and, to my questions, Mom had explained that only those who made the munitions and the weapons of warfare—the *industrialists*—benefited from the fighting. "Everyone," she concluded, "paid a price in loss of life and wealth—even the victor!" I realized some years later that this was a deeply held and inculcated belief in her people (the Jews of Eastern Europe), who were often the victims of violence and displacement, and led ultimately to their diaspora to the United States and elsewhere.

We didn't dwell on the foreboding situation in Europe during the early months of the war. The good years were continuing for my family, and work resumed on the house's interior, with finish carpenters cutting and fitting moldings, baseboards, chair rails, and the like. I would sit and watch

Mr. Baker, who was well beyond any conceived retirement age, cut and shape the built-ins for the kitchen, and hear him mutter, "'T'aint quite right yet" as he viewed his work. With few exceptions, built-ins at the time were fabricated on the spot, and the results might vary according to the whims of the craftsman. Mr. Baker gave my mom a very good kitchen with one exception: he constructed the cabinetry's depth using a dinner plate to calculate the measurement. The cabinet, to Mom's dismay, didn't accommodate her larger plates and platters, and later led to much fussing and exclamations of, "Damn, damn, damn!" She forgave Mr. Baker, however, as most of his work was exceptional. And, after all, "he was an old man."

Lorraine and Bobby had by now moved on to high school, and George Jr. had matriculated to junior high. The high schoolers had developed a swarm of friends; they were dating, their lives in full swing with a boogie-woogie beat. This was the big band era, and in mild weather groups like Artie Shaw, the Glenn Miller Band, Tommy Dorsey, and Hoagy Carmichael would tour New England, appearing at places like the Chateau in downtown Bangor. Their infectious rhythms were stimulating to the "bobby-soxers" of the late thirties, and on warm nights, the doors and windows fully opened, the old Chateau throbbed as the musicians hit a jazz tempo. 'Rainey's date calendar must have been enviable, even to her closest friends. She preferred dating boys "from across the river," she said, from John Bapst or Bangor High School. "They're more different, more grown up," she elaborated.

I inadvertently came across Lorraine's diary during these years and, to a degree, vicariously shared the new and exciting world she and Bobby were living in: which of their acquaintances was going with whom, which of them were "steadies," and revelations such as, "I don't like him, he smokes," or "She'd look better at school without lipstick!" Other comments I noted: "He thinks he's a communist (?)," and "Charlotte, Leita, and I stayed up half the night listening to Bing, he's really in the groove!"

It was surprising to me then—and still is—that she had such an extensive social life, considering she maintained top-of-her-class grades in school and worked Friday nights and Saturdays at F.W. Woolworth's Five and Ten. (By now, she'd moved on from Miss Alice Farrington's employ.) My sister forgave me of my intrusion into her diary—I'd stumbled upon it innocently enough—but she rendered me a stern lecture on privacy I've retained to this day.

Like Lorraine, Bobby had a great circle of friends. They, too, followed the band and dancing circuit, often taking road trips (usually hitchhiking), going "where the girls were." I have visions of Bobby, his cuffs rolled up one turn—the vogue then—his dark curly hair displaying a hint of Brylcreem, wearing a clean white shirt he'd meticulously ironed, and gulping down his supper, while his pals in somebody's borrowed jalopy awaited him out in the driveway.

At school, Bobby exhibited less interest in his academic studies than his sister, though he had acceptably decent grades. He much preferred the industrial arts curriculum where he could be more expressive of his talents. He loved his classes in woodworking and metal shaping, bringing home fine examples of his work, some of which he'd both designed and fabricated. I admired the Williamsburg sewing cabinet, with its intricate joinery and wood turnings, that he'd brought home to Mom and that stood proudly next to her Singer machine. A professional artisan would have given it his approval. I was fascinated as well by his engineering drawings—the carefully laid down lines and details, the exquisite lettering—though I barely understood the substance of those renderings. His work would contribute much to my later interests in art and architecture.

Bobby was complaisant in some respects about school, but he could be passionate in pursuing his own interests. By working after school at our local A&P Store (with as many hours as his schedule would allow), he obtained the means for a good social life. His busy life would not allow for participating in team activities—though he loved sports—but he found an alternative in which he excelled, boxing.

Jerry Dupres, a middle-aged former boxer, became Bob's coach and mentor. How they found each other I never learned. What Jerry found in my brother was a fifteen-year-old of short but muscular stature with a phenomenally hard punch and a lot of ambition. He would have taught Bob to constantly jab at his opponent, use feints and footwork to wear down and unsettle his adversary, and finding an opening, to slam home a vicious right cross or uppercut to the head, sending the competitor sprawling in the ring.

Boxing was a rough sport. Its appeal, in part, was its prize money. Bob hid this activity from our parents for several reasons: They would not have approved of the "sport" for their son, and he was not of sufficient age. Consequently, he fought under an assumed name, "Kid Garnier," Gon-yah in Maine speech.

Bobby was cocky about his fistic abilities and, when someone would yell, "Nice fight last night!" he'd nudge me with a friendly punch on the shoulder. It was amazing that in a bruising sport, Kid Garnier remained unscathed, never in my memory having brought home noticeable bruises from his boxing bouts. Our parents were destined to find out about Bobby's extracurricular activities, as his successes in the ring were rumored about town, and we siblings couldn't resist bragging about our big brother.

An offshoot of Bobby's ring experience was the construction of a platform to hold an official-sized boxing ring behind our garage. There, big brother would place padded mitts on our hands, give us rudimentary instructions in the "sweet science" of boxing, and let us flail away at each other. In late summer we'd dismantle the ring and erect a white canvas-walled tent, which sat comfortably within the platform's dimensions. We boys—all five of us—would place our sleeping cots there till cool weather and school days beckoned us back to the house.

For several years we split our summers, going to Hermon Pond for part of the time and spending intervals bunking down in the backyard, camp style, under white canvas. Our evenings, there in the darkness of the tent, remain some of my most fond and vivid memories. With natural light fading, Bobby would relate to us his adventures in summer camp. (As a young novice at Camp Jordan, the YMCA's summer establishment, Bob had so impressed the staff with his affable demeanor and his enthusiasm, that his two-week visit—all my parents could afford—was extended to the rest of the summer.) He'd teach us hiking songs and those lyrics from around the campfire that children forever bring home from their summer excursions. When true darkness enveloped us, Bobby and George, Jr. would alternate telling ghost stories. I'd crawl deep into my blankets where, pleasantly scared, I'd fall asleep.

"Well, what do you think, Ruth?" my dad asked, as Mom descended from the house, closing the screen door behind her. She stood just off the driveway and glanced approvingly at the picket fence that now surrounded the little bungalow on Chamberlain Street.

"It's our dream," she said, almost under her breath, surveying one of the finishing touches that symbolized the termination of home construction begun some nine years previously. "Pretty" and similar platitudes were seldom in her vocabulary. Her pleasure and admiration were most evident when she walked with Dad, arm in arm, circling the house, with her head at times on his shoulder and both thankfully quiet. For a moment they would forget the long struggles, the setbacks, and the disappointments that had accompanied their visions of home and family, the long road from Bayonne, New Jersey.

We children were mostly thrilled with our newly completed house and quarters. The living room with its abundance of bookcases, the dining room with a glassed-in corner cabinet that Mom had requested, and a kitchen agleam with Frigidaire range and refrigerator were cheerful and bespoke a family whose life was centered in its home. I was not ungrateful but less than thrilled, however, to have my cubbyhole above the staircase landing forever boarded and plastered in. I was attempting not to reveal my disappointment when Dad produced a wooden box, meticulously packed, with my possessions. As I happily accepted my things, Dad assured me, "You'll find another hiding place, and you can now put your books with mine in the living room." The latter suggestion indicated I'd risen a notch in my father's esteem, and I happily placed my Hardy Boys mysteries and my *Bounty Trilogy* alongside his histories of Napoleon and the Panama Canal.

I kept the box, adding my collection of lead soldiers, ship models, stamps, coins, "works of art," and the jackknives Hutch and I had retained—in contradiction to rules—and stuffed it into the far reaches of the toy closet. My hideaway had vanished, but I'd moved up in the world.

After a decade or more of heating homes with parlor and kitchen stoves, we now had a bona fide central heating system to ward off the cold New England winter. Surely, there are more charming elements in the home than its heating apparatus, but as a boy I found the "Iron Fireman," a relatively smallish furnace (by 1948 standards) and the nucleus of the system, beguiling. It stood proudly next to the chimney, its square body a textured red with contrasting black doors, adjacent to the coal bin. In some models, the Fireman could automatically shovel the fuel to the firebox, but that was not Dad's choice.

Returning from work, still in coat and tie, Father would appear in the basement to attend the Fireman, a ritual he reserved to himself and seemingly enjoyed. He'd check the fire and ash compartments and, with his left hand securely embracing the upper corner of the furnace, he'd shovel a measure of coal with his right hand, in a smooth, dance-like movement to the fire. In the morning, he'd repeat the process.

A charming affinity seemed to have existed between Dad and the Fireman. A few years later, when Father had passed on and the coal era had given way to oil, we connected the furnace to the new fuel, thereby eliminating the several-times-a-day stoking of the firebox. Yet there, where he'd grasped the corner of the equipment to steady himself, the enamel had been burnished to a glossy red, in vivid contrast to the remainder of the furnace's finish. It was a poignant reminder of his devotion to the heating system—the heart of the house in a New England winter.

The new furnace provided an additional benefit: it heated the ambient areas in the basement, creating comfortable play and activity spaces. On weekends, and sometimes in the evening, Dad would convert part of the basement to a shop, where he'd build or repair something, often inviting me to join him. We had youthful friends over frequently and we'd make "movies," using an old—now electrified—magic lantern which could magnify images onto a sheet pasted on the wall. At other times we'd create and enact silly little dramas to which we'd invite Mama, hoping for her assurance that there was talent there, waiting to be unlocked.

Poland had been overrun and a stalemate existed, the period later called the "phony war." Russia and Germany had concluded a Nonaggression Pact between their nations and, with the incentive to create a future buffer zone between itself and Western Europe, the Soviets had established control over the Baltic nations. They had also extracted concessions and territory from Finland, but only after extraordinary resistance by the Finns.

The quiet on Germany's western front was broken in April of 1940, when the Germans moved into Denmark and, almost simultaneously into Norway. If there was any question as to the limits of the Teutonic ambitions, it was answered on May 10th with the invasions, by land and air assault, of the Low Countries and of France itself.

The German offensive against the French avoided the Maginot fortifications and smashed, instead, through the Ardennes Forest, where it flanked and breached all French resistance and drove in *blitzkrieg* fashion toward the channel ports along the North Sea, in an attempt to trap Britain's Expeditionary Force. The belligerency of the Axis in Europe and Japan in the Far East was beginning to have its effect on American public opinion, and the pendulum was swinging away from "isolationism" toward "intervention," though cautiously.

With England under aerial bombardment, its fate unsure, Roosevelt had prodded Congress to prepare for the inevitable: We would most likely be drawn into a global conflict. Against a continuing notion among many in government, the media, and in public life, he convinced Congress to reestablish the draft, update our military, and gird for war. Against cries that he was dragging America inextricably into a European war, the President pushed an exchange of obsolete American vessels for the extended use of dozens of British bases. This was followed in early 1941 by the Lend-Lease Act (a subterfuge, in the minds of FDR's opponents), which circumvented neutrality laws and placed America in a position to exert new industrial muscle in the cause of free nations everywhere.

In Bangor, downtown was humming. Construction equipment rolled through the streets destined for Dow Field, the Air Corps base on outer Hammond Street, as airmen arrived filling the barracks. Homeowners were creating apartments in many grand old homes at the urging of local authorities to house families of servicemen who'd been called up from civilian life. The newcomers, many of them newlyweds, shopped and dined, walked and rode trolleys, all about the city. Downtown, soldiers newly arrived clustered at the street corners, taking note of the New England accents and the pretty girls giggling and dashing by. For a city well accustomed to a stirring downtown, there was a new and welcomed vitality that year.

On Harlow Street, Dad and the store's owner, JJ, were in deep conversation about what was occurring in Bangor—and what they were hearing from around the world—and how it might impact business locally. Quoting *The Wall Street Journal*, JJ read, "Many industries are curtailing productions of civilian goods and gearing up to produce the materiel of war." Continuing, he cited a letter on his desk: "I've a notification from the Frigidaire people that we should be aware of possible restrictions or limitations being placed on any of our future orders." JJ, usually consummately relaxed, one shoed foot with gartered socks resting comfortably on the desk when reading the *Journal*, had his feet firmly on the floor this day.

"What are your thoughts, George?" he asked.

"As I see it, we should place the largest order they'll accept! Enough to see us through till spring, when we'll be able to see our way more clearly."

They placed their order, went scurrying about town searching for secure, long-term storage, and held their breath.

Ironically, the previous two or three years had been rewarding years for my family—even as Europe convulsed, and our nation struggled out of a long economic depression, only to face a looming war. We'd finished work on our bungalow home and turned our attention to the cottage at Hermon Pond in the summers. Even with the specter of hostilities clouding the future, my family found comfort and opportunity in the moment. Mom began shopping for home furnishings (maybe even a new dress or two?), things she'd long ago denied herself. Dad longingly viewed the automobile ads in the *Saturday Evening Post*, saying, "We might just buy one of these...."

The stores in Bangor were generally open in the evenings until nine o'clock on Saturdays, and on one of those days, Mom took me with her, much to the chagrin of my brothers Floyd and Hutch, who were bade to stay home. I took my weekly bath, brushed back my crew cut, put on my linen blue slack suit with short sleeves, and walked with Mom the mile and a half to the Sears, Roebuck store. "Your father says you have good taste," she informed me, clueing me as to why I'd been chosen for the mission. I remember we selected a dining room set, maple and sturdy-looking, with clean lines. Mom arranged for a Monday delivery, and we left, traveling to "Dad's" store, which was next door. It was a warm, muggy Saturday evening, and both Dad and JJ were out on the sidewalk, jovially bantering with the passersby. JJ was always a very pleasant man, and he asked my mom, with a tone of amusement, "...and who is this little gentleman?" as he skimmed his hand across my "flat-topped" head. Dad beamed at us, placed his arms on our shoulders, and suggested we go to the Brass Rail, where he'd join us presently.

We set out for the restaurant passing numerous stores, their doors opened wide to the evening's air. As we strode by the Paramount Lounge, I showed Mom the sign on its door that read "Ladies Welcome." She chuckled, saying, "I don't know any lady who'd venture in there"—emphasizing *lady*. Fronting on Exchange Street's sidewalk, the Brass Rail's exterior was an exciting example of thirties-modern renovation (at least to a child), with gleaming circular windows, enameled panels, and bright chrome trim. Inside, the restaurant was in full buzz as we entered, the booths were packed with foursomes who'd been out on the town, and military personnel, mostly officers, finishing a quick meal before heading back to the base. Two young lieutenants, with pilot's wings on their blouses, gave us their booth. To my mother's protests they responded, "We have an early flight scheduled and need to hit the sack."

Having closed the shop, Dad linked up with us and, sitting next to me, put his arm around me, saying, "It was nice of you to come with your mother." I smiled at Dad thinking I was privileged to have been asked!

In a home of eight children, my parents strove not to show favoritism to any one of us. But it was inevitable, because of birth order, family necessity, or some mystic connection between child and parent, that somebody would be indulged from time to time. Conversely, one child might be more burdened, required to carry more weight than the others. The latter condition befell Lorraine, being the oldest, who routinely shouldered the task of rearing her younger siblings. On the other hand, if favoritism existed in our family, I received more than my share.

In the midst of these "better years," in 1939, my mother was summoned home to say good-bye to her dying father, Julius, (his given name Judah having been anglicized). It had been fourteen years since she'd last been to see family in Bayonne and, as grieved as she was to see her father slipping away, she made the most of it, catching up with her family and relatives and, in a modest way, "doing the town." Accompanied by her siblings and cousins, she toured the New York World's Fair at its height, on Long Island. In a world, much of which was not at peace, it was exhilarating to see the future—a prospect of beauty, technical and cultural advancement, and tranquility. She brought home a number of booklets of New York and the Fair, augmenting her many postcards to us. She even spoiled herself with a shopping excursion to Fifth Avenue with her cousin Celia. It was mostly a tour de force of window shopping, she later explained, but nevertheless stimulating "and a whole lot less expensive." To be there, to sense again the vibrations of a great city, was a consummate joy.

By the end of 1940, America's friend and would-be ally, France, had seen its military devastated and was now occupied by German forces in the north and reduced to a feckless Vichy government in the south. Britain, by dint of its new and pugnacious leader, Winston Churchill, and a heroic effort by a hastily assembled civil armada of small craft, along with elements of the Royal Navy and the RAF, had evacuated 340,000 members of the British Expeditionary Forces off the beaches of Dunkirk. As if to accentuate his success on land, Hitler ordered a massive aerial assault on Britain, raining down death and destruction, particularly on metropolitan London, in what would be called the Battle of Britain. England had now become an island fortress, alone against a seemingly unstoppable German war machine.

In Spain, fascist forces had prevailed, leaving Francisco Franco as head of state. Franco, both friendly to and cautious of Germany, declared Spain's neutrality in the ensuing conflict and was joined by its Iberian neighbor, Portugal, in that stance.

Italy had joined in the fracas, and Mussolini, having declared the Mediterranean "Mare Nostrum," had landed troops in Greece and Libya, and stormed ashore in Eritrea, where they were in a stalemate against an Ethiopian uprising. Il Duce had yet not made a declaration of hostilities against the United States or its allies, and there were hopes that he would not.

Japan continued its aggression in the Far East, had conquered the Korean peninsula, (which it recast as Chosen), Taiwan (Formosa) and controlled many of the coastal provinces of China, as well as Manchuria (Manchukuo). In response to Japan's belligerence, the American government had ordered an embargo on petroleum and metal commodities, though their full effects were yet to come.

Like an odd couple, Germany and Russia observed the German–Soviet Nonaggression Pact that provided a modicum of peace in the East, after Germany had demolished Poland. The couple stood, like unwilling partners seeking a divorce, each awaiting an advantageous moment to sever the relationship. Germany's notice of severance—early in the morning of June 2nd—was to send a massive column of Panzer tanks, followed by infantry, hurtling across the Russian frontier. Simultaneously, Stuka dive bombers screamed out of the skies, wreaking havoc on an impotent Red Army, fleeing in front of the invading ground forces.

The events that were shaking the globe and consuming its attention had an extraordinary impact on us children as well. Each day a new place-name would appear on the *Bangor Daily News's* front page or be the focus of a "first-hand report from the front" on the RCA radio that sat next to Dad's chair (and was considered a fine piece of furniture). We'd mull the new name over in our minds a moment and then laughingly try to pronounce it. Eventually, we would search it out in the atlas. Maps and charts had long fascinated me—almost from the time I could first read. There exists an almost magic illumination when tracing a material event to a spot at the end of your finger. Dad encouraged our interests and brought home large-scale, folding maps that Hutch and I would spread on the living room carpet, forcing others to step around us as we searched for the Ural Mountains or the Yangtze River. Semantically, there is a vast difference between "maps" and "territory." But to us, "real action" occurred at a point we'd traced on paper.

It was late April, the weather refreshingly balmy, after a blustery, late winter, and our family spirits were elevated as we contemplated summer vacations and Lorraine's high school graduation. By virtue of her final year grades, she stood at the top of her high school senior class. It was a distinctive achievement for a young woman, whose spare moment was spent working at Woolworth's department store or helping Mom corral and tame us younger ones. She had a multitude of friends, many of whom came to visit, and a heavy date calendar, though the "date," because of her schedule, might be little more than a walk home from work!

We were seated for dinner—the entire family, a rare event as Lorraine and Bobby often worked those hours—and a sparkle of good feelings pervaded the table. Not so with 'Rainey. She sat there without expression, silent. We'd finished our plates, which the older boys were collecting, and awaited a dessert of chocolate bread pudding, a favorite, when Lorraine suddenly spoke up: "Mr. Leighton (the principal) called me into his office."

"I'm *not* going to be the valedictorian! He said the honor would go to the *boy* with the highest grades. He said it was going to Donald Dinsmore!" Rainey was weeping by this time. I was confounded by the term "valedictorian," but I did understand the issue of grades. We all realized that our sister had been deeply hurt and offended.

We gathered around and hugged 'Rainey. She quickly composed herself and went on explaining, "Mr. Leighton didn't answer my question, *why?* He just mentioned I could accept the position of class salutatorian, but the school had always had a male as its class valedictorian, and 'I'm not about to change that policy!'" I'm not aware that Lorraine accepted his offer of second best. It would have been out of character for her to have done so.

There was an unquestioned article of fairness in our family: Women had their right to a place under the sun, of opportunity and success, as did men. But it didn't necessarily reflect attitudes beyond our household.

People might have sensed a fresh level of energy that summer, a quickening of the step like an up-tempo jazz beat. Once the cheers and commotion of commencement subsided, the graduates, taking little pause to contemplate their entry into adulthood, lined up for employment. There had been little anxiety over the previous two years of acceptances to college, as we've seen in more contemporary times. A small minority would go on to higher education, but the vast majority, following tradition, would go into the workforce. There were other paths such as the military or the Civilian Conservation Corps, and many young men, out of a sense of patriotism or perhaps a desire to get a steady paycheck, followed these routes.

During high school, Lorraine had brought home the requisite bulletins from Boston University and other colleges, though she knew her trajectory was to go to work. She intuited that college, if attainable at all, was sometime in the future. Hence, she went with purpose to the telephone company on Park Street and filled out an application for employment.

Across the country, National Guard units had been summoned to active duty. Locally, the 152nd Field Artillery Battalion, its members and gun batteries scattered around Penobscot County, mustered and commenced serious training. I watched one morning as the battery from our South Brewer armory assembled and, with commands echoing across the field, hiked in loose columns out Eastern Avenue. Wearing vintage campaign hats with rifles slung casually over their shoulders, they resembled Boy Scouts on a summer tramp more than troopers. They were certainly inferior to the Wehrmacht we'd viewed on newsreels at the movie house, and didn't inspire our confidence should we enter a shooting war.

The Bangor high school ROTC program, one of just a few units created at the secondary school level in the country, had produced qualified graduates for several years. While the accepted track may have been to matriculate through a college level program, the Army would shortly realize it had a store of eager, able-bodied younger men ready to flesh out its officer corps. Bangor would have an inordinate number of its high school graduates who'd be platoon leaders and company commanders in the combat that lay ahead. As attested by excelling grades among a broad number of conscripts during the previous war (World War I), Maine high schools would arguably produce more than their share of officer candidates for the Army and the other services in the next war.

We drove out Hammond Street in early July, the '37 Ford packed with children, parents, and boxes of groceries bound for Herman Pond and the good times of summer. The Pilot's Grill, whose entry was diagonally across from the air base's main gate, was much alive with people jamming the doorways, others standing about, as we motored by. The restaurant, owned by a Greek family, had become an unofficial extension of Dow Field and provided an affable meeting ground for civilian locals and service personnel. Continuing our trip west, we could see a multitude of aircraft—B-17 bombers and fighter craft—positioned wingtip-to-wingtip. It was an impressive sight, a measure of our nation's productive might, a tribute to a president who'd pushed and cajoled America into preparedness.

We were still a country at peace, though we were arming ourselves with preparedness. With sanctions and embargoes that stigmatized our potential enemies, Germany and Japan, we'd qualified our quasi-neutral stance. Who knew what eruption, accident or incident might shatter the uneasy status quo?

Time at the cottage was most pleasant, more than we dared hope for, considering the hostile world beyond us. Dad had formed "working parties" for his sons—all of us—on several prior weekends, and we'd painted, roofed and repaired screens and windows, producing a more esthetically pleasing and livable camp. We also improved the functioning of Mom's kitchen. "Bound to please her," Dad claimed. These days provided some of the few times Bobby was at Hermon Pond with us, as he had such a full schedule and life back in town. He'd cap every day with a long-distance swim, at which he excelled.

Our youngest, Ruthie (Ruth Marie) and Pat, now ages seven and five, were active and engaged children, but much less of a burden to Mom. She could pursue the newspapers and periodicals like *Time, Newsweek* and the *Post* in a more leisurely fashion and take part with us romping about on the beach or careening Half Pint. When time permitted, her favorite activity was long-distance swimming.

Clad in a single-piece black suit, her bathing cap tightly over her head, Mom would wade into the pond. When the waters were above her waist, she'd turn, ask us to stay well up on the beach to watch the little ones, and push off with a strong, rhythmic overhand. From the middle of the pond, over a half mile away, she'd wave to us and, without changing her repetitive stroke, swim off to her right for several minutes, turning again in a box-like pattern till she was back in mid-pond. She'd return to the beach, laughingly remove her bathing cap, and quip, "OK, everybody in the water!" She had swum nearly two miles with no visible fatigue, a feat I could never equal.

Throughout the summer, we'd engage in continual games, enlisting our visiting friends and even our little sister to obtain a quorum. I'd found Kenneth Robert's *Arundel* the spring before, and Floyd and Hutch would prod Mom to "get his nose out of the book" and come join them. I'd take my turn at bat or whatever and return to my reading as fast as I could. We became more capable of helping Mom with meals that summer, each taking our turn, and looked anxiously forward to Dad's coming each weekend. He'd surprise Mom with special things for our dinners, as well as a family favorite, chocolate doughnuts. Mom was at her happiest when Dad was with us. Their relationship, I observed, was more spontaneous at camp, less structured than at home.

During these good times, Lorraine and Bobby stayed in town with Dad working. 'Rainey had secured full-time employment with the New England Telephone Company, part of the Bell System, and was happy in her work. She had already advanced to a supervisor's position. Junior (George, Jr.) was with us in Hermon, though as a young teenager, he went off to work at a nearby farm most days. Junior had passed through pubescence and, like Bobby, had a well-developed, brawny physique. When, we younger boys wondered, would our bodies reveal those bulging muscular contours?

As ever, the summer went too swiftly, and we were back on Chamberlain Street at the end of August. By now, folks were considering removing the awnings that had protected them from the excessive summer heat, and children could be heard discussing who'd be their new teacher. Serious conversations, which had taken a hiatus in the warm, languid months, resumed and could be heard again in the streets.

Yet, Americans in large numbers continued to look inward. Who would win the next heavyweight bout between Joe Lewis and the German, Max Schmeling? Could Michigan win the Rose Bowl, if it won the Big Ten? And, of course, who do you like in the World Series—the Yankees or the Dodgers?

To more contemplative minds, the aggressive expansionism of Germany and Japan established an all but certain vector toward war. Though the British had defeated Hitler's attempts to bring it to its knees with an aerial assault the likes of which the world had never seen, and the Russians had stopped the German offensive at the gates of Moscow, the allies needed the Americans' industrial and military might to fully turn the tide. But Charles Lindberg and his American Firsters still railed against our involvement in the "other peoples' war."

There was a decisive outcome in the seventh game of baseball's championship series. Mickey Owen, catcher for the Dodgers, dropped the ball on the batter's last strike, in what would have been the final out in the contest. The error allowed the Yankees to continue on, eventually winning the Series. Hearts were broken in Brooklyn, but of little comparison to the hurt and humiliation America was about to be dealt.

At home, Mom stocked and canned fruits and vegetables for the winter and for a probable long season of discontent. Dad brought home super-sized cans of peaches, bags of sugar, and other commodities that, should hostilities erupt, would be in short supply. "No matter what happens," Dad explained, "we'll have to eat!" As his work generally required a great deal of travel, he put four new tires on the Ford. In just a few months these activities might be referred to as "hoarding," antithetical to the national effort of preparedness. For the moment, they seemed reasonable steps to protect one's family and livelihood.

On the first Sunday in December 1941, we pulled on our gum rubber boots, tugged stocking hats down over our ears and, with scarves flying, headed into the cold morning, bound for Mass. Junior was leading us with cousins Bobby and Sonny Dougherty joining in, and we all went into a half-run down the hill. We would receive Communion during the service and had gone without breakfast—fasting from midnight was still required at that time. Hutch and I, grumbling, made no secret of our hunger, and Bobby, probably more consciously Catholic than we, dismissed our belly-aching, telling us to be quiet.

After Father Moriarty had pronounced, "*Pax vobiscum*," we shared the blessing of peace, both liturgically and in a concrete worldly sense. Our country had been in a "state of emergency preparedness" for over a year. The question now was, would this be our last Sunday of peace? As I knelt for Holy Eucharist at the communion rail, I felt a sudden attachment to those around me, like we'd closed ranks. Not just in our parish, but across our nation we had melded, building a united front against any conceivable foe.

As we neared the hilltop on our return home, we noted a complete absence of snow in the fields and in the cow pasture. The brook however, that flowed and sloshed out of the pasture, was mirror-still, frozen as to allow a young person to jump and slide upon its surface, which Hutch and I did promptly without thinking about it. We caught up with Junior and the others, said good-bye to the Doughertys, and entered our yard.

Mom had breakfast on the table for us, the others having eaten. She always made a big breakfast for us on Sunday knowing we'd be ravenous, and our appetites didn't disappoint her as we dove into the eggs, the potatoes, and the grilled ham. Brother Bobby came bursting through the back door, he'd gone to the Post Office Square in Bangor and returned with Sunday's Boston Globe. There was generally a section for everyone who wished to read. I'd abandoned the comics a year or two earlier, since they really weren't very funny. Bob grabbed the sports and handed me the front section, telling me to bring it in to Dad.

The radio was on, though no one was actually listening to it, and Dad was about to light his cigarette as I handed him the newspaper and, finding no room on the sofa, settled on the floor between Father and the radio, I was about to reach for one of my books on the windowsill when the radio abruptly went silent, and then a grave voice spoke. "We interrupt this program to report that there has been an attack on Pearl Harbor on Oahu in the Hawaiian Islands. There has been heavy damage...loss of life. Carrier-based Japanese aircraft...still under attack."

Our entire family was now in the living room, completely stunned. Dad unconsciously laid the newspaper across his lap, displaying its headline, "Japanese Envoy Kurusu Continues Negotiations in Washington." I looked around at my parents, at my brothers and sisters. I didn't know it then but we'd never again—all of us—come together in one room.

The war, now global as we'd declared war on Japan, Italy, and Germany, was bound to cause lots of disturbances. On the surface, our home and our lives continued as before that awful Sunday. We went back to our respective schools and prepared for Christmas.

The older boys had erected an ice rink in the brickyard during the fall, nature had filled it, and by early January we'd tie on skates, gingerly cross the road, and waddle down to the rink. The news would travel that there was good skating at the brickyard, and dozens of kids, some we barely knew, would show up.

We were self-taught and not very good skaters, but we had a world of fun. One of our favorite games on the ice was "chorum." (Where that name came from or its meaning I never knew.) It was essentially a game of tag, lasting until all had been tagged. We often skated under nature's light at night. It made the games more elusive and challenging. It made skating more intriguing, I later learned, if a pretty new girl showed up.

As the weeks went by, more warplanes appeared overhead. Mostly B-17s, they'd fly almost directly over our house, with a roar of their four engines as they approached the base's runways across the river. As one plane disappeared beyond the tree line, another would resume its thunder, the crescendo reverberating for hours. In the morning a symphony of engines warming up on the runways would echo across the river. This low rumble would be rhythmically punctuated by a full-engine boom signaling another B-17 airborne, destined for Newfoundland and on to England and the war.

Each crew of airmen might be with us several days or just overnight. Most were pink-cheeked, the epitome of young American manhood, looking little older than brother Bobby. Our townspeople welcomed the short-term visitors with enthusiasm. They'd arrive in town by the busload. On Saturdays, in football season, they'd come by the hundreds to the games, cheering either or both teams. Dressed in leather flight jackets and pants with sheepskin lining, and wearing heavy low-cut boots and gloves, they stood among the locals, happy to be on the ground. Someone, usually a native son or middle-aged man, would whip out a flask of whisky and all—airmen and townspeople alike—would take a neat swig, wiping their mouths with their jacketed sleeve. It was a ritual that spoke volumes: we were all in this together!

An earlier contingent of servicemen had arrived during the previous months of the new base's opening. They were the cadre of specialists, the highly trained technicians, both officers and enlisted, who'd train others and maintain the aircraft. In many ways they were the nucleus of the Army's air corps. These men tended to be older and married, some accompanied by their wives and children. Many had been called up from the reserves, pulled out of civilian life. Most now would face reassignment to other bases around the country or to more distant places as the war widened.

Our parents befriended a number of these folks, sharing our home and, typically, Sunday dinner. One couple from Iowa came with their two-year-old daughter, Vicky and were an instant hit with us children. The husband was transferring to a unit scheduled for duty in the South Pacific. Our mom and his wife formed an almost immediate and lasting friendship. The two exchanged letters throughout the war and for years afterward. Another couple were being reassigned to Langley Field in Virginia, near their hometown. They established a quick rapport and affection with Lorraine. Our sister, who had shown a wanderlust since graduation, was enchanted when they suggested she come visit or even stay with them in their home near Hampton, Virginia. Within a year 'Rainey would move from our family to theirs—at least temporarily—carrying her job skills and work position to another Bell company. She'd be the first to leave our home on Chamberlain Street.

Having one of us say good-bye was a new experience for all. Anticipating her departure, and wanting every moment together, we'd ask 'Rainey to sing to us before going out on a date or other venture. She'd lovingly respond with a favorite, "Blueberry Hill," a simple but hauntingly lyrical ballad of lost love. When she'd finished and come "down" from Blueberry Hill, we'd beg for one more song, "Somewhere over the Rainbow." She would have admitted she was no singer, but her voice sounded angelic to us. The poignancy of her leaving was all too apparent.

Less than six months later, Bobby would graduate from high school. He looked promising and handsome in his yearbook. The rolled-up sleeves and pants cuffs of yesterday were gone, as he celebrated with the class of '42 in his new glen plaid suit, which Dad had helped him buy. Before the summer ended, Bobby, too, was headed to Virginia, where Lorraine promised Mom she'd keep a careful eye on him.

With our two eldest siblings away, life would be somewhat changed at home. We'd miss them at Sunday dinner, and we'd be deprived of their anecdotes of happenings around town, but the activity level within the house remained largely unchanged. Though Mom had cautioned them about life in the big world beyond Chamberlain Street, she trusted them to make good friends and insisted they write home. Both corresponded faithfully throughout the war years.

"The Camp" (cottage) at Hermon Pond.

CHAPTER 15

The smoke from the devastation in the Hawaiian Islands, Wake, Midway, and Guam had not cleared when the Japanese turned their attention to the Philippines, then an American territory. An archipelago of several large islands and countless smaller ones, the Philippines had been reinforced with tens of thousands of our air, land, and naval forces, even though many of our best military minds had advised against doing so. Following the destruction of our airpower, the Japanese came ashore in Northern Luzon Island, forcing the Americans into a losing struggle on Bataan Peninsula and, a few months later, crushing the courageous but doomed American resistance on the fortress island of Corregidor.

Our losses and disappointments continued almost unabated for the first six months of the war. We were rearming; factories that had produced Buick automobiles and Frigidaire appliances were turning out tanks, guns, and military Jeeps. Shipyards on all coasts were laying down keels for new destroyers, aircraft carriers, and Liberty ships to carry the cargo of war to our allies. But morale across the nation was at a low point. To lift our mood, stirring little songs like "Remember Pearl Harbor...as we go on to victory!" were played on the airwaves, and stories of individual heroism, many of them contrived, were circulated. We needed a real victory in the Pacific, and we needed it soon.

It came in June of 1942 in the Battle of Midway Island. There, 1200 miles west of Hawaii, an American task force under Admiral Bill Halsey met a large Japanese naval force and delivered a decisive victory. Our forces suffered some notable losses, but we inflicted a much more severe loss on our enemy, destroying a number of his aircraft carriers. We had given ourselves some breathing room. At the same time, we'd identified men, weapons, and tactics that would prevail in the Pacific War. Most importantly we'd handed the public something to cheer about.

Another small but significant boost to morale had occurred two months earlier, when sixteen B-25 bombers commanded by Col. James Doolittle of the Army Air Corps had flown over Tokyo, startling the Japanese though causing little damage on the ground. Launched from the aircraft carrier USS *Hornet*, it was both a bold display of American bravado and a heralding of the military might of an aroused and vengeful nation.

At home we were now feeling more effects of the war, as rationing of a great many commodities began, including most groceries and petroleum products. A small amount of grumbling aside, most citizens accepted the rations, allowances, and shortages as minimal sacrifices, making the necessary adjustments and going on with their lives. For larger families like ours, the rationing system allowed more flexibility than it did to smaller households. In our neighborhood, bartering reemerged, and loaning and borrowing were constants on the hilltop. As a next-door child's birthday approached, we might hear a rap on our back door and a request: "Could we spare two cups of sugar?"

The war crept closer to us as, one by one, the older boys went off to training camps. As neighbors, we became closer. We needed everyone to participate now that the older boys had left. It was not unusual for us to help the Dougherty boys with their chores, so that, in return, we'd maintain a full roster of the Hilltop Riders, our neighborhood baseball team. When hay harvesting ended in September, the Doughertys would invite the adjacent families to join them in a corn roast down in the brickyard. This was generous of them and an emblem of community spirit. It was done almost annually and young and old pitched in to set up a large bonfire, get the chairs for the parents, and cook, while keeping the little ones away from the fire as we nibbled and talked the night away. (For the adults, there may have been bottles of Pickwick or Ballantine ales, though I never saw visible evidence.) It also provided a good platform to celebrate the "new" adults on our hill and to those moving on to the service or a career.

For our family the cheering would be short-lived. We had enjoyed the summer hiatus at Hermon Pond as usual, but with the rationing of gasoline, it seemed unlikely we could maintain two homes in the future. At Dad's store the final order had come in and was inventoried. Their allocation was but half of what they hoped for. Meanwhile, the factory had gone over to war production. Dad and JJ would have another conference. I believe John McLaughlin cared deeply about Dad and our family, and he hesitated to relate what the near term foreshadowed. Dad knew when the current supplies were sold and accounted for, he'd be "separated for the duration" of the war. He offered his thoughts to JJ, and the two agreed on a tentative departure date.

Being a realist, Mom most likely would have reflected on Dad's dilemma well before his separation from the store. Typically, they hugged rather than cried. They'd been caught in a riptide before and they knew, instinctively, how to swim to shore, protect and succor their family. Dad's initial attempts to find work at a supervisory level were unsuccessful. Most employers, such as at a paper mill where he'd applied, required a physicality that he no longer possessed, or they included night and weekend work hours which would leave no time for family. After several months— and lowering his sights—he found what he was looking for, employment with the Hinckley Boat Yard in Manset on Mount Desert Island. The job offered several advantages; he'd be working with wood as a boat carpenter, a trade he well understood, and with coastal people he loved.

There would be a shortfall in family finances for a while, Mom warned—Dad's carpentry work would not fully compensate for his previous earnings—and she'd be more reliant than ever on our contributions for the summer. That year we saw Junior off to work at Sample's Shipyard in Boothbay, and Floyd joined a summer program that specifically aided bean farmers, where he quickly gained status as a "champion bean picker" and had his photo in the *Bangor Daily News*. Hutch and I acquired newspaper routes from the *Bangor Daily News*, rising daily at five thirty year-round and, in my case, delivering over a hundred newspapers before returning home for breakfast. Hutch had a similar route with slightly fewer customers adjacent to my territory. Should either of us be ill, the other would deliver both routes. (If we were really desperate, we'd enlist Ruthie, who was barely seven.) It was daunting work in winter. We'd be out in the biting cold for hours, our feet numb, as insulated boots had not yet been invented, even for the military. This provided incentive to finish as quickly as possible and get home to warmth and breakfast.

In the summer, except for rainy days, it was pleasant to be out on our routes. I'd read the front pages during my deliveries and chat with my customers, many of whom had family in the military. Many displayed a small red-bordered flag in their front windows signifying with blue stars each family member in the armed services. I tried to talk to all whose kinfolk were away defending our country. On some windows a gold star, symbolizing a death in the war, would appear. I would hesitate engaging lest I offend those in deep grief.

On Saturday, our paper bags were most heavily burdened. The *Bangor Daily News* was a six-day paper and the Saturday edition was the "Sunday paper"—all the features for the weekend, including the comics, were in that issue. I employed two bags strapped diagonally across both shoulders to handle my load.

With no school on Saturdays, we had a strong motivation to finish our routes as quickly as possible so that we might salvage time for a neighborhood game of baseball. Yet even that would be cut short as we needed to retrace our routes to collect for the paper, and in the afternoon settle up our accounts with the *News*.

For a youngster, the newspaper business was relatively rewarding; If I collected all that was due from my customers, I'd have a fiver in my hands at week's end. Hutch and I referred to it as soldiers' pay. (It was roughly equivalent to the twenty-one bucks a month a private in the Army might receive.) I learned to be cautious however, as some customers would stiff their paperboy. Though I did not personally experience that behavior, I did have to return on Mondays to collect from those few who just "didn't have the change!"

There was one quirk that I found unsettling. On the "better" routes, those with an abundance of fine homes, a percentage of deliveries were to "subscribers." Their papers were rolled and sealed with their name attached and their transactions directly with the company—though I made the delivery. As I didn't collect from these folks, I received no recompense— normally five cents per customer. In other words, I got stiffed by the publisher. I guess all is fair in love, war, and the newspaper business.

As more young men left for the service—draft ages had been dropped to eighteen and extended to forty—youth my age were welcomed by local farmers to gather and bring in the hay. In that first summer I took a job on the Wiswell Road, just beyond the town limits and a four-mile trek each way. A kindly older man whose only son was in pilot training, Mr. Soucy was well beyond retirement age, his stature slightly bent, but with arms and hands that still looked strong and capable. Sharing the work along with his sagacious directions, we brought in the crop within two weeks, a record he bragged about. His wife would insist I sit with them for dinner each day, which was served country-style at noon. Afterward we'd finish our haying and feed his flock of turkeys. I'd get a full dollar to pocket before hiking home.

On the Doughertys' farm, the need for young arms was even more acute, as between the two families, four of their sons had been called to active service. Their haying season would begin in June and extend well into August.

The farm had managed well, with mostly family help, for many years. The sole outsider was Harold, an iconic figure whose prominent brow and dark, deep set eyes spoke of some long-ago but lingering sadness. He was a capable farmhand who'd perform his work without comment and, at the end of the day, quietly disappear. But Harold couldn't compensate for the loss of four big boys. Sunny and Bobby Dougherty were shouldering more and more of the workload, though they were barely older than me. Once I'd finished with Mr. Soucy, they recruited me.

Building a hay load properly requires some basic knowledge of structures...and patience. The corners must be constructed before filling the middle of the wagon, and cooperation and timing with the crew pitching up to you is essential. My first load was a failure whose front corner collapsed and fell off the wagon on its journey to the barn. With experience I learned to alternate layering the hay in one direction with subsequent layers in the other, like a mason building a stone corner.

Before the summer ended, I'd worked most positions except driving a tractor. The haying fields were a considerable distance from the barn, some as distant as Gypsy Rock, and I enjoyed the trek back to the farm, standing on the gearbox behind Uncle Hugh as we pulled the loaded wagon with the Farmall tractor. I established an unusual rapport with Uncle Hugh, and we'd confer about world events, family issues, and even his personal health. Sometime later I discovered he'd confided in me about a terminal illness he may not have mentioned to his family.

We built strong, well-tanned bodies by the end of the summer—our upper bodies, that is, as we'd wear long pants to avoid itching and bruising from the dry hay. We would also build up a layer of dust and sweat each day. When the last load was securely in the barn, Sonny and I would head for an abandoned shed where we'd rigged a water-filled steel drum overhead, doff our clothes, and enjoy a lukewarm but refreshing shower. It was a rewarding end to a hard day's work, as welcome as the dollar I'd receive from Uncle Lou Dougherty before heading home.

"Dear Mom," the letter began. "I'm in the Marine Corps, and I'm on Parris Island." With that, Mother learned that our big brother had been inducted into the armed services. He went on to tell her they'd cut his curly hair—all of it—that the training was tough, tougher than he'd expected, the drill instructor demeaning and demanding. But the food was good! There wouldn't be much time to write, he went on, "We are training seven days a week, lucky to get an eight-hour sleep. No leave or liberty till we leave this sand-and-flea-infested island!" In closing he told Mom, "Don't worry about me, I can take whatever they dish out. Love, Bobby."

Finishing boot camp, his platoon members were assigned to various postings and obtained no leave time. "There's a war on," his D.I. informed the men. "You can ask for leave at your new duty station."

Bob (we decided to drop the "Bobby") received a temporary assignment to the naval facility at Indian Point, Maryland, from which he came home to us on short leave. Though Bob stood not more than five foot six, he looked virile and handsome in his summer khaki uniform. The Marine Corps was a good fit for Bob: tough kid, tough outfit! He developed a slight, but noticeable, swagger—convincingly more rugged than boastful.

Our brother would spend too little time with us, as he had a number of buddies also home on leave and several girlfriends to check in with. We enjoyed his brief visit—some ten days at most—and Dad brought him to the train station for another good-bye. Bob was transferred shortly afterward to Camp Lejeune in North Carolina for advanced infantry and combat training. He would be allowed one more short visit home before his unit would ship out for the South Pacific.

A short time after Bob's entry into the Marines, Lorraine's host family in Virginia saw the husband off for an assignment with the 8th Air Force in England. 'Rainey, not willing to be so far away from family, took a job with the telephone company in New York City. She had dreamed of New York (Mom was full of stories of old New York) and now, at age twenty, was living on the East Side, sharing a 6th floor walk-up with two other young ladies.

Lorraine immediately fell in love with New York City, as so many of the young do. She loved its fast, almost frenzied pace. She'd come down to the street—"always dressed and made up"—and hit the sidewalks in full stride. "If you linger, New Yorkers will shun you as an out-of-towner." In wartime, the girls opened their apartment to visiting servicemen from their respective hometowns. The women would double or triple up, allowing the young men to sleep over, often with blankets on the floor. "We'd have fifteen or twenty of us jammed into three rooms, a pot of spaghetti with red sauce bubbling away on the stove, and the guys anteing up money for beer." One such visitor was Jimmie Dougherty, our neighbor from Chamberlain Street, on overnight liberty from his ship tied up at the Brooklyn Navy Yard. It was as close to being home as many of them would get for a year or more.

American airpower had been steadily built up in England, and by late 1942 our bombers, along with those from the Royal Air Force, were conducting operations—limited at first because of lack of suitable fighter escort—over parts of occupied Western Europe. Major ground units from the States were assembling and training throughout Great Britain, as were their counterparts from the British Empire, its territories, and smaller groups from Occupied France and Poland.

When the assault on the continent was launched, it would be a true Allied effort. Meanwhile, as American military leaders were promoting the installation of a second front as soon as possible on the beaches of France, their opposites in the British High Command were in favor of more focused, divisionary assaults—"hit and run tactics"—until the joint armies possessed overwhelming strength, but delaying major engagement. Winston Churchill personally pushed for striking the "soft underbelly" of the Axis, in and around the Mediterranean. A compromise was ultimately arrived at; they would launch "Operation Torch" in North Africa as an initial move. When their flank in North Africa was secured, they'd move on to Sicily and Italy. A move against the Continent would still be a year or so away.

The German High Command had previously seen the advantage of controlling North Africa, the flanks of the Mediterranean Sea, and denying the British communication lines to its possessions in Africa and the Middle East. The thrust of "Operation Torch" was essentially to wrest French North Africa away from its Vichy collaborators, and to establish bases for the invasion of Italy and Southern Europe. It was primarily an American operation, and it went relatively well, with French forces—with the exception of its fleet—dropping resistance. In order to get the American force ashore quickly near Casablanca, much of the French fleet was sent to the bottom of the harbor.

Recognizing the precariousness of their position in North Africa, German General Rommel airlifted heavy reinforcements to the region. In several initial engagements, American forces operated poorly, unprepared as they were for desert warfare. In a short time, strong leadership in the person of General Patton, along with improved mechanized equipment and tactics, would save the day. Coupled with a renewed and regenerated British Army to the east in Egypt, the Allies gained ultimate victory and the surrender of a quarter million soldiers of Germany's Africa Corp. It was then on to Sicily and Italy.

With my older siblings moving on, and my being allowed more personal freedom, I began to travel about, exploring my surroundings in the two river cities that constituted my world: Bangor and Brewer and the Penobscot River that both flowed between and connected them.

For the timbermen of nineteenth century Maine, the waters of the Penobscot were the conduit for the heavy pine logs cut from virgin forests in the river's watershed and driven downstream to the sawmills of Bangor.

In a short space of time, the city became an acknowledged capital of the lumber industry, and a number of its citizens acquired enormous fortunes. These successful merchants, collectively known as the lumber barons, constructed palatial homes on many of Bangor's wide-avenued streets and set a tone of affluence that was still evident in the prewar years of my youth. A few of those barons gathered their wealth and departed for Boston or New York, but the pattern had been set: Bangor would become a center for commerce and industry, a thriving port city, and a city possessing cultural institutions that mirrored those of Portland and Boston.

The success of its neighboring town was felt in Brewer, though to a lesser degree. The inclined banks at the water's edge had caught the eye of Colonel John Brown a century earlier as an ideal spot for ship building. Here coastal schooners, built and pushed into the river from Brewer's shipyards, would carry the lumber produced across the way, along with bricks from Brewer's brick kilns, to the fast-growing cities along the Eastern Seaboard. When the era of sail died out, the yards shifted to constructing steam-powered craft. These early steamboats, still handsomely wood-planked, would ply the rivers, the lakes, and the shorelines of the Eastern United States for decades, until steel-hulled vessels superseded them in the early 1900s. With the cessation of shipbuilding and a fall in demand for bricks in the same period, the town experienced a slow decline, to where it became essentially a residential community.

As the fighting progressed in Europe, in Africa and in the Far East, Hutch and I resorted more and more to our maps. We would sprawl on the living room floor, life going on about us, and search for El Alamein in Egypt, Kasserine Pass in Tunisia, and the Solomon Islands north of Australia. We now had family in the war, but at times, we'd play a game of war on our maps, one of us assuming the role of the Germans. Hutch was good at that; he liked being a contrarian. (He even preferred the Detroit Tigers over our Boston Red Sox!)

The war was increasingly having effects on our family and those of our neighbors. It came as no surprise when our parents announced we'd not be going to Herman Pond that summer or anytime in the near future. Our newspaper routes would have precluded our going, in any event. Submarines operating close offshore all along the Atlantic seaboard resulted in a severe shortage of gasoline for civilian consumption, and Dad sometimes had to miss a weekend with us. Nearly every type of food was now rationed, as well as many kinds of clothing. We hadn't seen a banana or a fresh orange since the year began.

We had one advantage over many folks: We had a major garden—we were encouraged to call it a "victory garden"—so we seldom worried about "the next meal." It was there, next to the tomatoes!

In the depth of the war—1943 through 1944—Dad and Junior built a small shed in the back of our property, approximately where Grandpa Alex's cottage had been. Father brought home two piglets in the back of the Ford, and they were called Tom and Jerry. We loved to care and feed them. Mom, wisely, told Junior: "Don't let your brothers and sisters get too fond of the animals." We later constructed a shed with lots of south-facing windows for a small flock of hens, about which Mom had no words of caution but a reminder we need to take turns at caring for our "farm" and its animals.

By midsummer, with Junior down at the shipyard in Boothbay and Floyd away at "bean" camp, Hutch and I were the sole caretakers, at least for exterior chores: the gardens, the animals, the lawns, and what we called the "Tom Sawyer job," painting the fence. For good measure, we conducted a side business doing lawns for several families on Washington Street whose sons had gone off to war.

At one home, that of the Bishops, their son, a music major in college, had inherited the property—a tiny cottage at best—and commenced to gut the structure and install a large organ inside with pipes bursting through the upstairs floor and into the attic. Mowing his lawn was a grotesque experience, but one we made lighthearted. As Bill Bishop pumped and played dirgeful music, Hutch and I would take turns acting Frankenstein, while the other moaned and wailed as the chorus. Bill Bishop never gave us a tip.

Now a preteen (though nobody ever referred to us as that), I was starting to feel a self-assurance about who I was. I was also noticing, more acutely, the opposite sex. One Saturday morning I'd collected from my paper route customers earlier and set out for Bangor on my own. When I reached the news office on Exchange Street, I went in, found a young man, his Bangor High letter sweater worn inside out (that was cool then), and settled up for the week. I decided not to return home immediately and instead strolled aimlessly up to State Street, past the banks on either side, and ended up in Merchant's Square. I looked in the window of Dakin's Sporting Goods, where the cops had exchanged gunfire with the Brady gang. I read the newspaper clippings, now yellowing, that described the event. It seemed so long ago to me. By then it was noontime, and office girls, as we called them, were streaming into the restaurants. *Lunch*, I thought. *That's a great idea.*

I entered the luncheon store and sat on the only counter stool not occupied, between two attractive young women. They were having an animated conversation, and I felt I should move. "No, no," they said, continuing their conversation over and through me. They were very much like Lorraine's high school girlfriends. The young ladies kept on their chatter about work and boyfriends and all, sometimes clutching my shoulder as a point of emphasis. Preparing to leave, they reapplied their lipstick and smiled at me, as if asking my approval. "We hope you'll be back to see us," one said directly to me. And the other finished her sentence, "In a few years." They were joking, but they'd made my day. The waitress, petite and smiling, finally took my order and observed, "So you like older women!"

People on the homefront were urged to do their part throughout the war years, and we youngsters aspired to make our contributions. Our town would periodically mount a paper drive or a collection of aluminum or tin cans, items to be processed into reusable commodities in the war effort. I had entered the Boy Scouts by then, and I'd take our little red cart, sometimes enlisting Hutch and little sister Ruthie, and ply the streets of Brewer being a good scout, helping to win the war! It was also beneficial to the ecology of our community, a recycling activity well ahead of its time.

To the very young, like my five-year-old sister Patricia, the war was a very local and frightening affair. For Patsy, the Germans were in Doughertys' Woods. It may have seemed far-fetched when she first proclaimed it, yet one of my Hardy Boys novels depicted a clandestine Nazi airfield smack in the middle of an American forest. Patsy would refuse to accompany us to the woods till well after the war. And who could blame her?

My Parents, Ruth and George Landry, c. 1943.

"Mr. Businessman," age twelve, during the war years.

CHAPTER 16

Mom received a short letter from Bob. His unit had concluded its training in North Carolina, had ridden on a troop train across the country (and a portion of Mexico), and were now in a tent city at Camp Pendleton, California. "It's orange blossom time here," said Bob. "Don't guess we'll get to see them." Indeed not, his Company G, 2nd Battalion, 22nd Marine Regiment was to board a ship the following day in San Diego. "My next address will be somewhere in the South Pacific!"

The troop transport, in a convoy of twenty other vessels with almost as many destroyers and light cruisers in escort, had been at sea nearly two weeks, stopping only to refuel and take on more personnel in Pearl Harbor. After steaming to the south a few days later and approaching the Equator, the ship's captain and the marine battalion's commanding officer decided the troops and the ship's company needed some diversion and a little entertainment. An event featuring King Neptune and his entourage would be celebrated at the precise time of their crossing the Equator, hour 1736 (about five thirty in the evening) two days later. It would be followed by a main event, a boxing match in the early evening before sunset and darkened ship conditions.

The events promised to provide a welcome break for the marines, whose routine had been one of training, calisthenics, and standing in a continuously forming chow line. (The vessel served only two daily meals, the lineup for the second meal commencing as the first meal was ending.)

Private 1st Class Robert Landry and his rifle squad had just concluded a strenuous twenty-minute drill with weapons when his platoon leader, Lieutenant Scott, pulled him aside. "Landry, the CO wants you to take on the Navy in the boxing ring day after tomorrow. You up to it?"

"Yes, sir," Bob replied, without a consideration of who he'd be fighting, or that he'd have little time to prepare.

Bob managed to steal away for a few hours, bringing a friend as a sparring mate, going below deck and acquiring boxing gloves from the ship's "athletics department" storage compartment. They donned the gloves, with Bob's partner holding his open hands up for Bob to swing at. They practiced through a number of five-minute rounds of fast punching and dancing about the passageway. He'd never felt more fit, Bob told his friend. His stamina, his timing, and his punch were like the old days under Jerry Dupuis. He was ready for whatever the Navy threw at him!

The ship's deck had been cleared, sailors and marines all about, as King Neptune (the ship's navigating officer) and his motley-dressed collection of Royal Attendants came up from the deep (below decks), frolicking in outlandish costumes to the howling amusement of hundreds of servicemen. Once the equator-crossing antics had ended, the captain announced a two-hour break till the featured event: "a boxing bout between Marine Bob Landry and our Navy's Dick Raymond."

The transport was plowing ahead at twelve knots in a moderate sea, leaving a broad wake behind. The sailors, other than those on watch, and the marines came up from the mess deck below and walked forward to the improvised ring beyond the ship's bridge, hoping to get the best seats for the fight. Like a football game between service academies, the ship's company was directed to the starboard side, the Marines to the port.

The Marines are part of the Navy, its most venerable branch, a fact that is acknowledged in combined formations where the marine detachment is placed forward and to the right. The Corps, by tradition, obtains a select group of Naval Academy graduates each year—those who may choose the Marine Corps. Yet down in the ranks among the enlisted men, there is a dichotomy of appreciation and antipathy for the Navy. The clash of two gladiators this day would be audible, amplifying that those feelings were still alive. It would all be in competitive good fun, however, on this day in the South Pacific, as the history of the two services is replete with heroic sacrifices sailors and marines have extended to each other.

As fight time neared, the ship began moving through areas of moderate swells, pitching from time to time followed by a noticeable rolling.

Yelling, "Gangway!" the ship's chief bos'n led the boxers and their seconds through the crowd. The fighters and their attendants climbed through the ropes, followed by the referee, as the spectators took their places on the deck, the ladders, wherever they could view the fight. The battalion sergeant major was Bob's trusted assistant and he helped the "hope of the Marines" lace up his boxing gloves. Diagonally across, Boats was serving as Raymond's attendant and in like fashion tying on the gloves for the red-headed sailor, the "pride of the Navy."

As a small rub of petrolatum was applied to his face and chest, Bob surveyed his opponent: "He's a couple inches taller, maybe ten pounds heavier. His face has been bruised, like a street fighter. Probably fights like a windmill, got to watch out for his wild swings."

A bell was rung, the fighters got up and went to the middle of the ring. The ref explained a few rules, had the contestants shake hands, and commanded them to "come out fighting!"

As another bell sounded, the boxers danced about in the ring feinting punches, probing for an advantage or a weak spot. The redhead then waded into Bob, his fist flying madly. "Tie him up, tie him up!" the sergeant major yelled. Bob went into a clinch with his opponent reducing him to flailing at empty air. They broke away before the referee could part them, and Bob got in a solid punch to the ribs. They traded blows for a while, and Raymond let loose a wild swing that grazed Bob's cheek. The sailor had chased Bob around the ring, not having landed a solid hit, and was panting when the bell ended Round One.

In Round Two Bob modified his strategy, becoming more aggressive, but watching for those crazy, wild swings. Dick Raymond was visibly less active, almost dragging his feet. Bob got in a strong left jab to the chin and followed it with a hard right—not to the head, as the sailor expected—but again to the ribs. When Bob approached again, Raymond let down his guard as if to protect his torso, and the "hope of the Corps" unleashed a salvo of punches to his opponent's head. Raymond was in trouble, and, instead of tying up Bob as a well-trained boxer might do, he slid along the ropes with Bob pummeling him at every step. A deafening roar came up from the portside of the ring (not quieting until long after the round ended). The redhead backed into a corner and Bob delivered a *coup de grâce* with vicious lefts and rights to his victim until he was on the deck. The round-ending bell sounded before Raymond could be counted out.

Boats had the smelling salts out, and the sailor was responding. He sat on his stool, but the fight was clearly gone out of him. The chief threw in the towel, signifying his client could not go on.

Bob had bounced up and danced to the middle of the ring as the referee threw his right hand into the air. "The winner by technical knock-out, Private Landry of the Marines." The marines exploded with cheers and pounded on the deck, and many of the sailors politely applauded along with them.

Bob went over to his opponent's corner, where the two hugged, exclaimed, "Good fight!" and wished each other well. All smiles, he went back to the compartment where his platoon bunked and got under a well-deserved shower. When he emerged, his buddies brought him back dinner and a cold beer they'd finagled from "somebody in the rec department," contraband aboard ship, no doubt, but refreshingly tasty.

The regiment was delivered to the Solomon Islands, for additional jungle and combat training. From there they tracked other Marine units, which had wrested the Marshall and Caroline Islands, Truk, Saipan, and finally Guam from the Japanese. Bob's regiment, still in training, was charged largely with mopping up the enemy who had slipped into the hills.

During 1943 and 1944, Hutch and I were studying our catechism for Confirmation. I began to see the human side of Father Moriarty when he offered to help my mother buy our handsome dark suits for the occasion. He'd done so numerous times for our family, as I think he did for others as well, though I never knew about any of this till many years later.

Father Tom Moriarty led an isolated, nearly monastic life, as did most priests in small communities. St. Joseph's rectory, where he was the sole resident, was comprised of a moderately sized Victorian house, almost elegant with its ashlar-shaped wood exterior, and an attached carriage house—now a garage—that stored the priest's black Buick sedan. He was loyally attended by an elderly, maiden woman named Margaret, who was his housekeeper, cook, and protector. Nobody could see "The Father" without proceeding through Margaret. She kept an immaculately clean parish house, tolerating neither dust nor sin nor unwarranted disturbances.

I had numerous occasions to visit the rectory, where Margaret, peering through heavily lensed glasses, would intercept me as she stood in the kitchen ironing the priest's shirts or altar linens for the church across the way. She'd summon Father Tom, who'd come smilingly into the kitchen, slipper-footed and black-vested but without Roman collar, to receive his visitor.

On Sunday summer afternoons, having finished his priestly duties, we often observed Father Moriarty driving past our house on Chamberlain Street. He'd be dressed in black suit and collar, with a straw hat sitting jauntily on his balding head. He would be on his way to the little farm on Pierce Road, run by Margaret and her equally elderly spinster sister, where the two "old biddies" (an affectionate Irish term) would entertain him with dinner and, most likely, a glass or two of spirits.

When learning that several older acolytes were leaving, I felt inspired and offered my own candidacy, roping in Hutch and Phil Day for good measure. (I guess I needed support.) It took us several months, working with Father Tom, as we privately called him, to learn and commit to memory the Latin then essential to the Catholic Mass. We felt truly accomplished when we could recite the Apostles' Creed in that beautiful classic language. A knowledge of Latin, I later learned, is of immense value when studying the Romance languages of Europe. Perhaps half of our English words, too, have a Latin origin. Our learning was rote, as we didn't fully understand the context or the subtleties of the language, though we had our little prayer books for a general translation.

We often served as altar boys on weekday mornings, as well as Sundays. We had to hustle through our early morning paper routes, make the seven o'clock service at church, rush home for breakfast, change clothes, and go to school. Father Tom rewarded us for our dedication by allowing us to serve at weddings, where we were paid handsomely by the wedding party.

It was late in the winter of 1943 that the casualty list from the war hit close to home. Having read the Epistle and reflected on the readings, Father Moriarty rose and went to the altar rail. He briefly wiped a bead of perspiration from his brow, placed his handkerchief in the sleeve of his white alb, and with arms crossed under a brocaded chasuble, or outer garment, he paused to begin his Sunday sermon. He would sometimes glance at the front pews where young boys and girls sat, apart from their parents, and would speak out sharply if he observed misbehavior. He didn't see anything out of line, but the corner of his eye picked up an usher rushing toward him.

Moriarty didn't tolerate disturbances to the order of the Mass—unless he initiated them. The usher was persistent, however, and when reaching the altar rail handed Father a message. He didn't hang around.

Father Moriarty viewed the note, took a breath, and read: "This note is to inform you...that Thomas Kane has been killed in action...." He hadn't finished reading when a dreadful cry came from the back of the church, and then another. It seemed like our whole parish was mourning. I don't know why the notification was sent to our church. It was a painful reminder of the toll war was taking across the country and in our town.

Tommy Kane had been a close friend of Bob's throughout high school, had visited with us countless times, and was well-liked by Lorraine as well. Hardly a week would go by without the loss of some young man our family knew.

As the weeks and months went on, the war and its broad sweep became ever more grim, reaching down to nearly every household. When young men reached eighteen, whether they'd finished school or not, they'd be drafted within a few weeks. Men with families, even those over forty, were drafted and compelled to serve with much younger, more physically fit conscripts. One such man, a neighbor whose house on State Street we could see from our home, was drafted, received minimal training, was shipped overseas, and his wife received notification of his death from the War Department, all in less than one year.

Russia had pleaded for a Second Front on the Continent to lessen the Nazis' capabilities on its Eastern Front. America had supplied and sustained the Red Army for over three years and had seen it grow to an impressive force, pushing the Germans back to the Dnieper River and inflicting heavy losses on the Germans in men and materiel.

American and British Air Forces, now with long-range fighters and bombers, extended the aerial war to most of Germany, as waves of bombers with fighter escorts raided the centers of war production day and night.

We had driven the Germans out of Sicily, given them savage battle in southern Italy, and with the siege of Rome, had seen Mussolini's government collapse. Germany occupied and assumed control of the rest of Italy, while a temporary leadership, for all intents and purposes, moved Italy to our side. The Nazis offered a continuing stiff resistance to the combined British and American armies, and the casualties mounted.

The "soft underbelly of Europe," as Churchill described it, was not particularly soft or yielding.

On Guam, the 22nd Marines were joined by two other regiments. Along with additional armored and support units, they would form the 6th Marine Division and would be leading the assault on Okinawa in the Ryukyu Island chain, an integral part of Japan.

CHAPTER 17

In Great Britain, the Allies were assembling a force of 2.8 million men to cross the English Channel and assault the beaches of France, creating a Second Front. Not since 1588 had an invasion of any great number been across that twenty-plus miles, and that attempt by the Spaniards had ended in disaster. The components necessary for launching this latter-day invasion were gathered in the English countryside and its ports, the soldiers trained, the tanks and artillery pieces readied and tested, and eleven thousand planes to supply air support sitting on the runways. The landing site(s) and tentative striking time had been agreed upon at the highest levels. All that was needed was the will to commit thirty-nine divisions to a violent reception.

On June 6th, I was up early to pick up my allotted newspapers at Hinkley's Drug Store, where the news truck dumped them off about five o'clock every morning but Sunday. As I pulled my papers out of their wire-bound bundle, the headline proclaimed: "Allied Invasion Force Lands in Normandy." In what would be known as D-Day, we had finally engaged in "the beginning of the end of the war," as Churchill put it. Within a few days, we had established a fifteen-mile-wide, seven-mile-deep beachhead with nearly 400,000 men and armed vehicles ashore. The fighting would be furious with German resistance stiff in all sectors, but the Allies were on the Continent and there to stay.

As I made my rounds, most of my customers came out to intercept me. They'd heard the news from a neighbor or from the radio and were anxious to learn if a friend or family member might be among those in the fighting. Father Tom, wearing his biretta, was dashing across Holyoke Street, his black cassock flying after him, as he sought to open the church for worshipers. He implored me, "Leave the paper with Margaret." My last customer was the Dougherty Farm, where Uncle Lou, in his usual attire of overalls and white undershirt, met me in the milk room. He'd heard the news too. He was perspiring as he offered me a bottle of milk to take home. (We exchanged the milk for the newspaper.) He then drank a swig of Pickwick Ale he kept in the cooler, chasing it with a mouthful of whole milk. At home, Dad was up listening excitedly to the early news on the radio.

We brought out our maps again: Cherbourg, St. Mere Eglise, Caen, Saint-Lo. I was taking eighth-grade French, and I would ask Miss Hall about the many sites our troops were moving through. She had visited and studied in some of these places, and I could feel her distress when she described how Normandy had been before the war. The game of war was losing its luster for me as I gazed on the photography of a war unfolding in France and the bloody carnage it was leaving behind.

The war had raged on in 1944 on multiple fronts in Europe and the Pacific. For me, the year meant a return to eighth grade. Junior high presents a moderately big transition for most children. Instead of being closeted in one room and one teacher, the students now move by subject matter to their teacher. Teachers are generally more learned in the course's content, and homework becomes the norm rather than the exception.

In Brewer, junior high was part and parcel of the high school system. We shared their teachers, coaches, gym instructors, and the offerings of shop (industrial arts) for the boys and home economics for the girls. The latter courses were utilitarian with practical application in family life—but have regrettably been dropped in most schools today.

There was a multitude of new faces—and characters. Most of us were naive and not quite of dating age. We'd just not reached that stage of maturation, at least most of my friends and I had not. But I did briefly acquire a girlfriend named Myrna. Her family owned the town's largest milk processing company, and her modest parties were joyfully braced with bottles of chocolate milk. I was most likely a reluctant suitor (I needed training and experience), and Myrna shortly moved on. A more long-lasting and invaluable friendship was finding a buddy in Donald Tracy. We were lifelong friends, both altar boys at St, Joseph's, and would follow each other to John Bapst High School and even the Marine Corps.

A number of kids came to school on buses from South Brewer, a largely blue-collar part of town. The boys were more street smart, more rough and tumble, who knew how to snitch a beer and engage with girls. The girls from South Brewer seemed prettier, more friendly and uninhibited. For better or worse, I'd learn a lot from my South Brewer friends.

Our school graded numerically and I continued making high grades, seldom slipping below 90. I could easily finish my homework during study period. I would have developed better study habits, however, had I been compelled to bring my work home. (I suppose what this would suggest is to improve performance, eliminate study periods!) During this transitional period, many of my old chums drifted off, some going to private schools, others moving away. My new friends were high-spirited, most athletically inclined, and not academically motivated.

George Jr. had turned eighteen over the summer and had entered into his senior year. He was focused on his schedule when Mom handed him the letter: a notice that he was to report for induction into the Armed Forces of the United States. It was a bitter moment for Mom. Young George was still a high school student, and a significant contributor to our family's finances. With two sons in the military, her thoughts must have replicated that proverbial utterance: "Old men start wars that young men are called to fight!" Not too many weeks later, Junior was off to navy boot camp. Bob had previously written from the South Pacific: "Go Navy. You'll have a clean sack and three squares a day!"

With the Japanese navy weakened and American airpower ascending to rule the skies, General MacArthur, commanding Pacific ground forces, and Admiral Nimitz of the Navy met with President Roosevelt, and the three agreed to an imminent invasion of the Philippine Islands. In Leyte Gulf, where Magellan had sailed some four hundred years before, elements of the US 6th Army splashed ashore in the early hours of October 20th. Before the day ended, the renown General, wading ashore, proclaimed, "I have returned!"

There would be many more land battles that fall that preceded a secure Philippines, but Leyte was a solid and forceful beginning. At sea the Navy extracted revenge for its losses at Pearl Harbor in several huge engagements, devastating the Japanese fleet wherever the two powers collided.

Herby Blakeley, our postman dropped it off. A thin, flat box, it held a recording that had traveled through several government channels to reach us. We placed it on the Victrola. It was Bob's voice. A news correspondent was interviewing several marines as they were being transported in a large strike force, and Bob was among them. His voice sounded confident, relating he'd be in the first wave in the coming invasion of Okinawa. Would they be scared? "Sure!"

There had been frightening casualties in the Pacific, as the Marines and Army had pushed, "island-hopping," toward the Philippines and Japan itself. We could only pray that our brother would survive the first day. The date of the invasion was not revealed, so we would worry unceasingly until we once again heard from him.

The Allies, under General Eisenhower, were steadily throwing the Germans out of northern France, albeit with heavy casualties on both sides. On the northern flank of the invasion force, British General Montgomery had initiated a campaign, which if it had succeeded, would have allowed the buildup of a quick thrust into Germany. It didn't succeed; in fact it stalled out, contributing to great loss of life in a combined British, American and Canadian force. Earlier, over the Christmas season, the Germans had mounted a last-ditch counteroffensive, which became the Battle of the Bulge. It failed but only after some surprising initial achievements. It indicated that there was still a lot of fight left in the German Wehrmacht. But overall, the invasion was going well, even ahead of the planning, and Paris had been liberated to great joy in late August that summer.

In desperation the Germans launched a new and terrifying phase of warfare: unmanned missiles aimed at London. The first weapon, the V-1, was a somewhat clumsy jet-powered weapon that would drop on London when it's fuel gave out. The V-2 was a true missile, rocket-powered, nearly invisible to the eye, and immensely destructive. Priority was soon given to bombing their launching sites and overrunning them on the ground. Had the Germans initiated this type of warfare earlier, it may well have changed the course of the war.

By year's end, our Allied armies were on the initiative on all fronts from the Netherlands to the Swiss border, ready to plunge into Germany.

On Easter Sunday, April 1st, four American divisions stormed ashore on Okinawa, including Bob's 6th Marine Division. Fortunately the Japanese defenses were light and sporadic on the beaches, the Japanese having learned over a long Pacific campaign the futility of wasting its resources opposing the landings. As our forces moved inland, the Japanese defenses stiffened and the land battle became intense. Bob was in the midst of this for several weeks when he wrote us a brief letter confirming where he was and that he was well, so far. As the Marines approached Shuri and Yonabaru near the Okinawan capital of Naha, the ground fighting became ever more fierce, some of the most intense of the Pacific war. Military planners in Washington were seriously pondering what our losses might be if and when we put our forces on the Japanese home islands.

Once across the Rhine at Remagen and encircling the Ruhr, where 350,000 German soldiers surrendered, the Allied juggernaut, with spectacular hammering assaults by American General Patton's armored divisions, spread out across the Fatherland. Toward the end of April, the western Allies were at the Elbe River, and the Russians were readying a final thrust on Berlin in the East.

Nothing, however, could have prepared our soldiers, or those at home, for the revelation of the death and torture camps uncovered as our forces drove toward Berlin. The depravity inflicted on Jews, young and old, and on those the Nazis judged to be enemies of the state, was jarringly ugly and audacious to the minds of all humanity. It was all but unviewable to Hutch and me when we saw clips of bodies piled like cordwood. That incredulity is with me to this day!

The atrocities, the development and use of horrendous weapons, the indiscriminate targeting of cities had totally changed the complexion of war in our young minds. We begin to fold and put away our maps.

The victory we were contemplating in Europe was tempered by the death of President Roosevelt on April 12th. He had brilliantly led us out of a severe economic depression; he had rearmed a reluctant, isolationist country against inevitable hostilities; and he had marshaled our armed forces, along with our Allies, in a global struggle that was just now approaching its conclusion.

Father Tom was no friend of Roosevelt, nor of the Democratic Party. *Too socialist*, he might have thought, or *too close to the Russians and their godless ways*. When I questioned him about Harry Truman, who'd be succeeding FDR, he replied "He's even worse!" Truman had not been "in the loop" among our wartime leaders, yet he'd have to finish the war on all fronts and guide us into the peace. He would redeem himself with a low-key but distinctive guidance on all accounts.

In the glare of sexual scandal that has rocked the Catholic Church, as well as other religions and institutions, it must be said that no evidence, fact or fiction, has emerged that would link Father Moriarty to such despicable misdeeds. As altar boys we would have been vulnerable to such abuse, but we were also a repository for rumors and gossip within the parish. Wrongdoing, or even the whisper of abusive behavior, would have alarmed and astonished us, leading to almost certain disclosure. This is not to say that Father Tom was without fault. He loved his whiskey. It was most likely his resort for dispelling loneliness imposed upon him by his vows of poverty and celibacy. He never drank or misbehaved publicly, and, more importantly, his imbibing never affected or detracted from his performance as a priest. He was, however, stopped once or twice by the local police for "being under the influence." In those postwar years, breaches of the law for this behavior were so common in society that no official action was recorded.

Conversely, Father Tom, from every facet I knew of him, would have resented the abuse and vile comportment and vocally railed against it and its attendant cover-up with every ounce of his moral being. He was fond of criticizing (though quietly) those among his higher-ups who might pontificate to others but, he judged, misunderstood the faith of ordinary church-goers. His barbs directed to the "powers that be," were sharp and targeted, frequently to those "across the river" in the large parishes of Bangor. He would no doubt have drawn the attention and scorn of the Bishop of Portland, Maine.

Father Tom may not have been a role model for other priests, but he was no hypocrite, either.

On the front lines in Okinawa there was a sadness knowing their "Captain" had died and some trepidation over who was steering the ship of state. Bob had heard rumors of the collapse of Germany. "Is it true?" he asked in his letters. His company had sustained heavy losses over the five weeks of continuous combat, we'd later learn, and his writing revealed a tone of deep fatigue.

His following letter, several weeks later, told us: "I've been wounded, evacuated to a hospital ship that is headed to Hawaii." He later wrote that he'd suffered "a concussion, with broken eardrums." He experienced a loss of hearing several days before his company commander, seeing blood running from his ears, relieved him and sent him to the battalion aid station, where he was evacuated. It was bittersweet news, but we knew Bob would be coming home.

Destiny hung over Europe as the German High Command capitulated and the firing stopped on May 7th. A formal surrender was signed the following day, May 8th. America celebrated, but cautiously. Within weeks, army units, reorganized and reinforced, were awaiting transport to the Far East. There was, after all, another war still going on.

The potential and dangers of atomic fusion had long been known in the scientific world. In 1939, several scientists, including Albert Einstein and Enrico Fermi, approached President Roosevelt to warn him of the dangers should Germany develop atomic weapons for war purposes, which would pose a catastrophe for the rest of the world. Roosevelt had taken the warning most seriously and had set in motion scientific and engineering initiatives to, hopefully, achieve the development of an atomic device before any other nation. By mid-1945 an atomic bomb had been tested, made available and was on its way to the Pacific on the venerable cruiser USS *Indianapolis*.

At a meeting in Potsdam, Germany, the American and British heads of state had presented an ultimatum to Japan: Accept a complete surrender and an Allied occupation of their homeland. Should they refuse, President Truman had set a timeline for the possible use of "the bomb": any moment after August 3rd. When Japanese Prime Minister Suzuki responded that the Potsdam Declaration was unworthy of the Japanese government's consideration, the die was cast. On August 6th, over Hiroshima, a weapon was detonated, obliterating four square miles of the city and some sixty thousand people. Three days later, with no movement toward surrender, a second device was exploded over Nagasaki. A surrender by the Japanese followed on August 14th.

Bells in church towers were ringing, neighbors excitingly calling across the street, as Hutch and I pulled the little red cart we thought we'd outgrown to the crest of the hill, jumped aboard and headed we-didn't-know-where to celebrate. Main Street in Brewer was already jammed with the townspeople, and we blended in with classmates and older citizens, motorists going nowhere but applying their horns, and one lad with whistle and cowbell—sounding off with both. It was maddening and spontaneous, a swelling comic relief from the burdens of four years of war.

The author at age fifteen, displaying a measure of self-assurance.

*"I did smoke—occasionally—as a teenager. However,
by the age of thirty, I'd permanently ceased. My best advice
on smoking: Don't start! It's a losing proposition."*

CHAPTER 18

Hutch and I were tending our victory garden, picking the last of the corn and a few beets for the table, when a deafening roar filled the sky above. We watched with great excitement as a stream of Boeing B-17s—the Flying Fortress, core of the 8th Air Force—came thundering down, their landing gear extended, for an arrival at Dow Air Base. They were returning to the States in a series of flights from England and the Continent. We cheered and waved madly as the crewmen, as emotional as we, waved back. It was a noisy but crowning moment to the war's end.

There was a collective joy in the streets of Bangor and Brewer that late summer. There was anticipation of reunion with family members who'd traveled away from us to give battle to our enemies. There was a tangible expectation of a lasting peace and hope of a new world order: nations living peaceably with their neighbors, and an institution to ensure that security. Most importantly, there was confidence that children could gaze into the skies without fear of bombs and missiles descending upon them.

Dad's employment at the Hinckley Boat Yard had ended—well before the end of hostilities—and he and Mom engaged in frequent conferences about what lay in the future for our family. "We'll be opening our own appliance store," Dad eventually announced. "It'll be right here in Brewer. We've picked out a spot, but we'll not be in business until we're assured our suppliers have resumed production. That could be several months. Until then," he went on, "we'll need everyone's help to get our venture started."

In the interim, Dad noted, there was a lucrative market for servicing older appliances and that "service" would be the cornerstone of a successful appliance business in the future. We shortly had a garage full of old ranges, washers, and refrigerators waiting for a second life.

This would indeed be a family project. When asked, both Hutch and I volunteered the war bonds we'd acquired through hard work on our paper routes. We truly had no plans for spending them, and we consoled ourselves that we'd merely transferred a "promise" from the Federal government—not money! When Floyd was asked if he'd follow, he hesitated. He mumbled that he'd "picked a lot of beans in the field to get his bonds and that...." He finally relented, "I guess if my brothers are giving. But it's only a loan!" Floyd's reaction was quite in character. He was cautious, and every "bean" was an asset.

Hostilities may have ended, but there was a palpable uneasiness in much of the world, particularly in Germany and in the countries of Eastern Europe which had been overrun by the Soviet Union. Germany was to be divided into four zones, with American, British, and French zones in the West and a Russian zone in the East. Berlin, deep in the Russian zone, was to be similarly divided into four sectors with free access guaranteed for all parties. The arrangement relied upon the good faith and cooperation of the occupying nations to achieve pacification, deliver humanitarian assistance, and rebuild war-torn Axis countries.

Cooperation was not forthcoming from the Russians. Though they had accepted the peace arrangements, they immediately began to extract reparations and a cruel revenge upon the defeated Germans. They systematically dismantled and removed machinery and equipment from the factories, imprisoned German scientists, removing them to Russia and, in Berlin, allowed its troops to conduct a rapacious campaign against women of all ages. Their behavior in the countries of Eastern Europe was no better, where they rooted out, killed, or imprisoned suspected democratic activists. Within a few short years of the war's end, Winston Churchill, speaking of Russia's failure to work in concert with her allies, their introduction of barriers to the peace and reconciliation of the conquered nations, declared that an "Iron Curtain" now existed between the Western Powers and the Soviet Union. It—the Cold War—would be in place for some four decades.

On the other side of the world, there was unrest in China. It should be remembered that in the interest of China, the United States had enacted embargoes upon the Japanese Empire as punishment for its aggression against its neighbors. This ultimately led Japan to attack us at Pearl Harbor. Now, Generalissimo Chiang Kai-Shek, whom we'd supported since the 1930s, was losing his grip as the Communists, sustained by Russia, were gaining strength and belligerency.

In Southeast Asia, Indochina, ostensibly controlled by France, was experiencing an insurgency by the Viet-Minh, led by Ho Chi Minh. Ho had valiantly fought the Japanese and was now fighting the colonial French for the region's national independence. Ho Chi Minh had initially admired the United States, hoping to imitate America's evolvement from the British Empire in the late 1700s. When his early efforts were rejected by the Paris Peace Conference of 1919, he looked instead to Russia for patronage.

And in Korea, where we'd encouraged Russia to join us in an all-out war against the Japanese in 1945, there was dissension over the division of the country, the North, aligned and occupied by Russia, and the South aligned and administered by the United States.

A more pleasant turn of events was occurring in Japan, where the American military under general Douglas MacArthur proceeded with sole power to rule over a newly structured Japanese government. Wisely, we had retained Emperor Hirohito, and with his consent and nearly godlike image, the Japanese people were passively accepting rule by the occupying Americans.

In San Francisco, the framework of a United Nations was being formed, and there was encouragement that there would emerge an acceptable vehicle for cooling the passions arising from efforts to establish peace and restructuring of our defeated enemies. There was optimism also, that the shortcomings of Woodrow Wilson's League of Nations could be avoided and that methods of opposing the use of force—and a means to collectively combat it should it occur—be instituted. The United Nations, as eventually confirmed by the Senate of the United States, would have its defects, but it was a brave new beginning.

The war had ended some months earlier, when a black, once-elegant 1930s Packard Coupe drove into our yard. And there was brother Bob and his recent bride, Grace. We had an exuberant and joyous reunion, even before the couple could enter the house. Bob looked healthy, tanned, and vigorous, with no visible scars from a terrible war. (There were scars but they were internal, some of which would plague him for decades.) Grace, a North Carolinian from the tobacco country, was acceptably attractive but not (in my opinion) a Southern beauty. She would find her way into our hearts, nevertheless. The two would stay with us for less than a week and, regrettably, leave to live in another world in Hampton, Virginia. It was the beginning of a trend: Having seen much of the country and the world, our older siblings would be restless, their restiveness quenched by moving along.

Lorraine, too, would come home—briefly—but always return to New York. She'd eventually "migrate" to the West, and we'd seldom see each other. Whenever she was with us, however, she would arrive bearing gifts, looking like a movie star, and full of good cheer. She never failed to mention that I was "her" baby!

As we enjoyed the return of our oldest brother and sister, George Jr. was outward bound to the Philippines, where he'd serve for nearly a year on a Landing Craft Tank (LCT), removing the materiel of war and ferrying supplies and personnel about the islands. He'd become fond of the Navy, liked his shipmates, and planned a career in the service. "I really love this life," he wrote to us, and he loved the Philippines and the beguiling Filipinas.

It looked as though having a diminished family was another casualty of the war.

On an August weekend in 1946, Mom suggested I go upstairs and "say good morning to your Dad." When he wasn't working, Dad savored the early hours by sleeping in and, upon waking, have one of us fetch and light a Raleigh for him.

Reaching his room, I could see that Dad had propped himself up with an extra pillow and set there comfortably, anticipating my lighting his cigarette. Exhaling the first "delicious drag," Dad alluded to the exodus of our older siblings and said he understood how we felt. "Things are going to get better, for all of us," he declared. He must have been speaking intuitively, not factually. Opening a family business, a daunting venture at best, was still months away, and though we'd not had the loss of a family member during the war, we'd suffered numerous privations including having to sell our summer cottage, Dad's sporadic employment, and foregoing luxuries and amusements and out-of-town trips.

Dad motioned to a copy of the *Saturday Evening Post* resting on his end table. As he brushed back his blond hair, I observed an advertisement for an Oldsmobile sedan, bright with color, proclaiming: "Powerful luxury, seats six with comfort!"

"I want to take you boys to Boston, and we'll see the Red Sox play. I want to take you to New York, to Philadelphia." He was almost giddy with excitement. We'd come through hard times—the Depression, the war, months, even years, where he'd been laid-up, out of work or under-employed. Yet Dad never lost his faith that "things would get better." He and Mom shared that inexplicable optimism that, if you could withstand the worst thrown at you, you'd "reach those sunny uplands," stronger in mind and heart for having survived the crucible. I'm sure I believed my dad that morning. It was just a matter of hard work and application—and optimism!

"But today," Dad said, "I'm going to take you (me, Hutch and Floyd) on an adventure!" Under wartime rationing we'd seldom left town except to help a nearby farmer bring in his hay or rescue his bean crop, and the mere suggestion of going anywhere unleashed pent-up emotions.

Mom admonished us to bring our jackets—"It'll be cool near the ocean"—nearly let the cat out of the bag. So, I rationalized, we'd be going east, toward the coast.

"Yes," Dad intoned, "I'm taking you to Acadia, to where I spent the last couple of years." He was referring to Mount Desert Island, but his refer-ence was to the coastal region thereabouts, as well. Dad loved to pull little surprises and he simply shrugged when Mom divulged part of his secret.

"I hozey the front seat," Floyd declared, using a local expression for staking out one's turf. Hutch and I settled in behind close to Dad, where we could chat easily. We drove out Chamberlain Street to State and headed Down East." Reaching Ellsworth, we detoured momentarily, to allow Dad to show us where our family had lived, briefly, in the late twenties before any of us had arrived. "Alsworth," as we called it, had a bustle to it that late August, with townspeople thronging the sidewalks in its small downtown, lawyers, briefcases in hand, dashing to the courthouse, and "early birds" seeking lunch in the cafés on Main Street. Dad sensed our own hunger but reminded us we just finished breakfast. He promised we'd have a "nice lunch" someplace along the way. "This is just a side trip," he told us as we drove on to East Blue Hill. "And this is a place your mother loves."

We returned to the Bar Harbor Road and proceeded to Trenton, which was then an isolated stretch of highway, level haying fields and green forest. There were several farm stands and hawkers on the side of the road and we stopped to pick up baskets of blueberries. "Just raked them this morning, down in Cherryfield," the hawker told us. Hutch and I stored them in the back of the Ford, and we continued on.

As we drove by the airfield farther down the road, Floyd pointed out the road to the Stuarts' cottage, where he'd spent time the previous summer and where I'd joined him for a weekend. Back in Brewer the Stuarts were on his paper route and, like many of our news customers, had befriended their youthful carrier. John Stuart was the local manager of the New England Telephone Company and respected and admired in the community. John and his wife sincerely loved their Scotch whiskey and intensely loathed the English. The airfield, almost adjacent to the cottage, had been largely given over to the British for training their pilots in this country, far from the endangered skies over England. The flight path, however, was frequently over the small cottage. When, on takeoffs or landings, they growled overhead, John would shake an upraised fist at them, his cheeks ruddy rosettes. When Floyd and I were not exploring the many coves and boat-building sheds along the shore, or planning to put a homemade cannon—a device made of springs with a modified Molotov cocktail—on a raft to drift out into Frenchman Bay and encounter a Nazi submarine, we'd climb to the "crow's nest" in the Stuarts' cottage and listen, with great amusement, to John's letting loose with his colorful invective just below us.

As we neared the bridge to Mount Desert Island, we were traveling abreast of several lobster pounds that dotted the highway and catered mostly to out-of-state visitors. "Would you like a taste of lobster?" Dad inquired.

"No," we chorused. Lobster, though special to our summer visitors, was not a commodity that excited our palates, at least at that time. Give us clams, cod, or haddock. Few of us had a taste for that crustacean—the lobster.

Once across the bridge, we drove toward the town of Bar Harbor, with Dad pointing out places of interest as we moved along. "There," Dad offered as we passed an attractive set of buildings, "is a gentleman's farm." In these parts it's usually called a saltwater farm. "I'm hoping we might acquire our own such place, sometime before your mother and I are too ancient to enjoy it." I learned that such a property would, in essence, border the shore and that it would serve more as a retirement home than an active farm. It would be another of Dad's dreams, to be attained, as he put it, "if we live long enough!"

Motoring by an impressive structure looking more institutional than inhabited, Dad explained it was the Jackson Laboratory, a place that bred mice for medical research and science and shipped the creatures worldwide. I instantly thought of Mr. Bradstreet, who'd commented, "If you continue with biology next year, you'll get your very own mouse!"

"So, they all will be killed," I asked?

"I suppose they will, but they'll be treated mercifully. It will benefit all of us through medical science." We thought silently about that tradeoff for the next several minutes.

Entering the town of Bar Harbor, we pulled off at the Acadia National Park headquarters on Cottage Street, where we procured maps and brochures of the park. We spotted Sand Beach on our map and noted it was just south of the town. "Can we go for a swim?"

"Of course," Dad answered as he went on to relate how the Rockefeller family had gifted the beach to the park in the 1930s. The family's generosity had indeed benefited Acadia National Park, and therefore the public, with numerous bequests of land, carriage roads and many smaller but beautiful structures.

Sand Beach is a typical barrier or pocket beach, created by the grinding and deposition processes of glacial activity and then sculpted, textured, and toned by wind and wave. A small meadow or salt marsh exists behind it, and a steep hill rises to its south. While much of the island consists of granite cliffs dropping down to the sea, here is an unexpected deviation: a jewel of sand and minuscule shell fragments beckoning young and old to test the waters.

To say that we went swimming would be an exaggeration. The waters were numbingly cold, but a few degrees above freezing, or so it felt. In any event, we'd not brought our swimming gear, so we "tested" the water up to our knees telling Dad it was "refreshing!"

The island is nearly half national park, though there is a sprinkling of villages along its parameters, and lakes and mountains seemingly everywhere. Leaving the beach, we drove on Route 3 toward Northeast Harbor. This region of the island is replete with fine homes and a scattering of more palatial houses, collectively referred to as "cottages." But Bar Harbor, as the entire island is sometimes called, is not Newport (Rhode Island)! Though in both areas the summer people—those with wealth and social standing—had similar intentions of escaping the oppressive heat of metropolitan cities, the Newport families tended to bring their urban opulence to the cool, breezy shores. The Bar Harbor people, in contrast, were *rusticators* much in the spirit of Teddy Roosevelt (though he was personally content with Long Island, NY). The rusticators relished the hiatus from the sophisticated rigidity of New York and Philadelphia and embraced the natural delights of Mount Desert Island as they found them. There were, of course, many exceptions in both cases, but the houses they built and the social customs they maintained bear out this divergence.

Entering Northeast Harbor, Dad pointed to various driveways, mostly understated (no elaborate columns or stony lions), but with an occasional peak at a splendid shingle-style home leading to the water. If the wealthy were "camping out" here, they were doing so with elegance, and good taste. We rode through the town's main street and followed Sargent Drive north, along the rocky edges of Somes Sound, a large, fjord-like inlet that effectively divides the island. Rounding the sound, we headed to Southwest Harbor on Route 102 and Dad, winking, asked, "Are you hungry?" We laughed as Dad said we'd eat in Southwest. When we reached the downtown, Dad pulled up to a nondescript wooden structure on the town's main street. Southwest Harbor was then, and perhaps still is, a working, blue-collar town, with an emphasis on boatbuilders, fishermen, and storekeepers. It was a charmingly honest small village, with little intrusion by outside people.

"I hope you like fried clams," Dad said. He needn't have asked us, as we hungrily piled into the restaurant. The main item on the menu—fried clams—was apparent, even from the street. We ordered a platter of the delicious shellfish, along with french fries and salads, though nobody ate the salads. Several townspeople came up to our table as we dug into golden brown, crispy mollusks.

"Hello, Georgie," one old hand uttered, as he grabbed Dad's shoulder. "We been missing you!" Others quickly followed suit, and it became apparent that Dad felt at home with these people and they with him.

"You gotta try Evelyn's blueberry pie," the waitress suggested, and we did. As we left, Dad bought yet another pie for us to tuck into the car. "Mom won't have to bake us a blueberry pie this Saturday," he crowed. That was true, but we also knew that the blueberry, in any form or concoction, was his favorite food. We stepped out of Evelyn's restaurant, our bellies satiated, to voices trailing us: "George, you gotta bring the wife down here!"

We slid into the Ford, and Dad drove about another mile, over to Manset and the Hinckley Boat Yard, where he'd been employed during the war. The foreman, recognizing Dad, let us in. We'd barely stepped into the yard, when there in front of us, stood two beautiful sailing craft up on ways, awaiting their anticipated launchings. Unhesitatingly and without thinking, Dad approached the nearest vessel and ran his hand appreciatively over its hull planking. (This was still a time before the general use of fiberglass.) "Nice work" he exclaimed to the foreman, and the two exchanged comments on the uniqueness of "Hinck" yachts, how their lines contributed to the dependable handling and smooth sailing.

"The owners will be here next weekend. Gotta a bit of work to do on the brightwork before then," the foreman said. "Gotta be in Bristol shape before the launch!" He then led us inside one of the huge boat sheds where several gray-clad Navy PT boats set elevated, partly covered. The contrast of these craft with the gleaming white sailboats we'd just viewed was like War and Peace.

"There's a market for these boats," the foreman assured us. "Gotta get the Navy's clearance to sell them. Lotta people want 'em."

"Well boys, these boats are a little too big and powerful for our Herman Pond," Dad said amused. The foreman allowed us to climb aboard and inspect one of the craft, and Dad explained how he'd worked on these boats and similar wooden vessels over the war years.

Reluctantly, we had to leave, but not before Dad and the foreman had chatted about the old days.

We returned to Route 102, retracing the road around the sound and headed east toward Hulls Cove on Frenchman Bay. Dad had one more surprise in store for us, though he chose not to disclose it till we were closer in. Meanwhile, we skirted Bar Harbor and traveled over one of the park roads, viewing mountains on all sides, before descending to Route 3. There are several park roads in the eastern portion of the island and a dozen or more unpaved carriage roads that penetrate the interior of the park. Each of them, their edges marked with large, rectangular granite stones quarried there on the island, provided a jeweled panorama of mountains, forest, and sea.

Driving up Route 3, we caught views of Frenchman Bay gleaming on our right. Dad's surprise was "something spectacular out on the water!"

Nearing the dock just south of Hulls Cove, we could see several small green islands, seemingly floating on the blue of Frenchman Bay. And then, "I see it, Dad! It's a huge warship!" Indeed, it was huge. It was gray, massive, and majestic, riding at anchor a mile or more out in the bay. It was the battleship USS *Missouri*, at war's end the queen of the Pacific, her decks glorified by the signing of the peace with Japan just eleven months earlier. "Are we going out to visit it?"

"Yes, yes! That's why we are here!"

After we parked, Dad urged us to get in line quickly. "I'll be right along," he said. We joined with several dozen others, mostly families, and watched for the launch that would carry us out. Dad walked down from the parking lot, waved to us, and stood back talking to a chief petty officer who seemed in charge of the operation. I couldn't discern their conversation, but with Dad's love of sea and ships, I knew it to be most likely "navy" talk.

"The boat's coming in," Floyd shouted, and Hutch repeated it. I left the line and stood before Dad, realizing in that instant that I was nearly as tall as he. And I also realized, with great disappointment, he'd not be going out to the ship with us. I wanted to plead with him, but his glance conveyed a finality that was not arbitral.

Dad broke away from the chief, placed his hand gently on my shoulder, and said, "I'd love to, but I know I'd have too much trouble negotiating the gangplank on and off the ship." I was almost in tears. We'd had so little time with Dad over the war years! As he firmed up his grip, I knew he empathized with me. "I'll make it up to you in other ways," he promised. He added, encouragingly, "Your mother and I are extremely proud of you boys. You may still be lads, but you've each done man's work over the last couple of years. In our eyes you're young men! You'll be just fine, going out on your own."

Descending the plank ladder to the launch, I turned to see Dad lean back against the railing and reach for a Raleigh in his shirt pocket.

"Shove off, Coxswain," the chief yelled, "you're loaded." We seated ourselves near the stern of the launch, with Floyd and Hutch talking excitedly about what they'd see on "Big Mo," as the Missouri came to be called. I was more reflective, happy I'd held back the tears. The helmsman placed the boat in slow reverse, pushed away from the dock, then smartly executed a 180-degree turn, heading into the bay.

When we were a few hundred feet away from the dock, I glanced back to see that Dad had turned seaward, the cigarette still clutched in his hand, unlit, his eyes on the horizon. His gaze spoke volumes to me. He was not expressing regret at being left ashore, but an intense and mystical pride at having launched three promising young men on their own life's journeys. I waved a feeble hand he doubtfully saw and settled down, feeling a new contentment. The coxswain executed yet another turn to accommodate the wave action and pushed the engine throttle forward. The launch began a rhythmic slapping as it plowed through the moderate swells, sending a soft, stimulating salt spray glancing off our faces. We couldn't talk over the engine's clatter, though I must have been beaming with happiness as Hutch and Floyd signaled me the two-fingered V for Victory, the WWII equivalent of a high-five. I remembered Dad's alluding to us as "young men." I intuited that maturity was a process: We were outward bound, and we were on course.

THE END

EPILOGUE

George William Landry, Sr., 1901–1947

My dad, George, Sr., would not live to acquire a salt water farm, nor would he attain the shiny new Oldsmobile. He did, however, establish an appliance business that stood successfully on Penobscot Square for nearly fifty years. "The good die young," he often said—and he did, at the age of forty-five.

Ruth (Ginsberg) Landry, 1905–1991

My mother, Ruth, had little time to mourn the loss of her husband. She had to preserve her home and family (there were still five children at home) and rescue a fledgling business. She would prove capable at every task, drawing the admiration of the community. In her later years, her health and memory declining, she loved holding my hand and listening to piano music, be it by a noted composer or just one of her grandchildren.

Lorraine Elizabeth (Landry) Veves, 1923–2005

'Rainey married, moved west, and with her girlish good looks wore Levi's every day and mingled with a Hollywood-type crowd at night. When we last spoke I was still "her baby."

Robert Eugene Landry, 1924–2012

Bob overcame many obstacles to obtain his engineering degree from the University of Pennsylvania (his dream), though he worked full-time, frequently at night, while enduring periods of migraine headaches stemming from his wartime injuries, to do so. Till the end, Bob remained my "big brother," especially when we were "doing the town" together.

Floyd Donald Landry, 1930–2016
Steady of character (maybe a bit rigid at times), Floyd retired as a colonel from the Air National Guard achieving the highest military rank in family annals.

Howard James Landry, 1933–2004
Smart and a superb athlete, though slim of build, Hutch loved a competition, whether on the field or in professional engineering. Unfortunately he'd lose in his challenge with smoking, too early in life.

Patricia Irene (Landry) Connolly, 1936–2013
Patsy followed her husband's Navy career, teaching in the public schools along the way. Like our oldest sister, Lorraine, she chose the West, retiring to the Sierra Mountains east of Sacramento.

Two of my siblings, **George Jr. and Ruth Marie**, remain with me. They and I are living in Maine—for me in the summers—maturing gracefully and enjoying our status as grandparents.

Contemplating the future, while considering the past: If, as reasonable men and women, we resolve to have peace instead of armaments and conflict, we will obtain it. If we elect to have a national economy that is fair, equitable and stable and a world that respects all nations and individuals, we will achieve them as well.

ACKNOWLEDGMENTS

Initiating my memoir, I assumed it would be a solitary and, occasionally, lonely venture. It has been that at times. But, if one writes in long-hand as I do, he relies on others to transpose his work to the computer and, eventually, on to the publisher. Thus, my manuscript became a team effort. (The writing, though, is entirely mine, and any mistakes in it are mine, as well.)

On the matter of teamwork, I've been more than fortunate. In Florida, where Roz and I maintain a *pied-à-terre* along the Indian River during the winter, there was Amy Morse, who gratuitously rendered my writing to the process, doing so for two years or more. There was, also, Christina Darragh who helped. In Maine there was Kit Reno, who put aside her own projects to aid me, and later, Joanna Boeing Bratton, who greatly assisted me, as we plowed through revision and editorial sequences. Angela Percival and Olivia Stilas provided timely assistance, as well. I had the benefit of several readers: Jack Landry, Caroline Janover, Clare Brett Smith, and Belvanne Prycl, whose comments were most useful. Along the way, I utilized the services and resources of numerous libraries, including the Maine State Library in Augusta, the Bangor City Library (Maine), and the Indian River Country Library in Vero Beach, Florida. Libraries, thankfully, remain our guardians of the printed word.

Lastly, I wish to thank my partner, Roz Allen, whose encouragement and support has kept my manuscript alive and flowing.

ABOUT THE AUTHOR

If Maine is in your blood, there is no washing it away. After an adult life spent largely in other places, Paul Landry returned to the ocean, the rivers, and the small towns of Maine for retirement. Paul is a graduate of the University of Maine, having attended Colby College as well, and possesses a work background of corporate business, entrepreneurial ventures, and teaching. He has six children and eleven grandchildren. An avid hiker, gardener, cook, and artist, Paul lives with his long-time partner, Roz (Rosamond Allen), in midcoast Maine on—of course—a river.